SEARCH FOR

AND OTHER

by

HANS HOFMANN

A monograph based on an exhibition, covering a half century of the art of Hans Hofmann, held at the Addison Gallery January 2—February 22, 1948

Edited by

SARAH T. WEEKS *and* BARTLETT H. HAYES, JR.

ADDISON GALLERY OF AMERICAN ART
Phillips Academy, Andover, Massachusetts

PUBLISHED WITH THE ASSISTANCE OF
THE ADDISON GALLERY ASSOCIATES

Copyright, 1948
BY THE ADDISON GALLERY OF AMERICAN ART

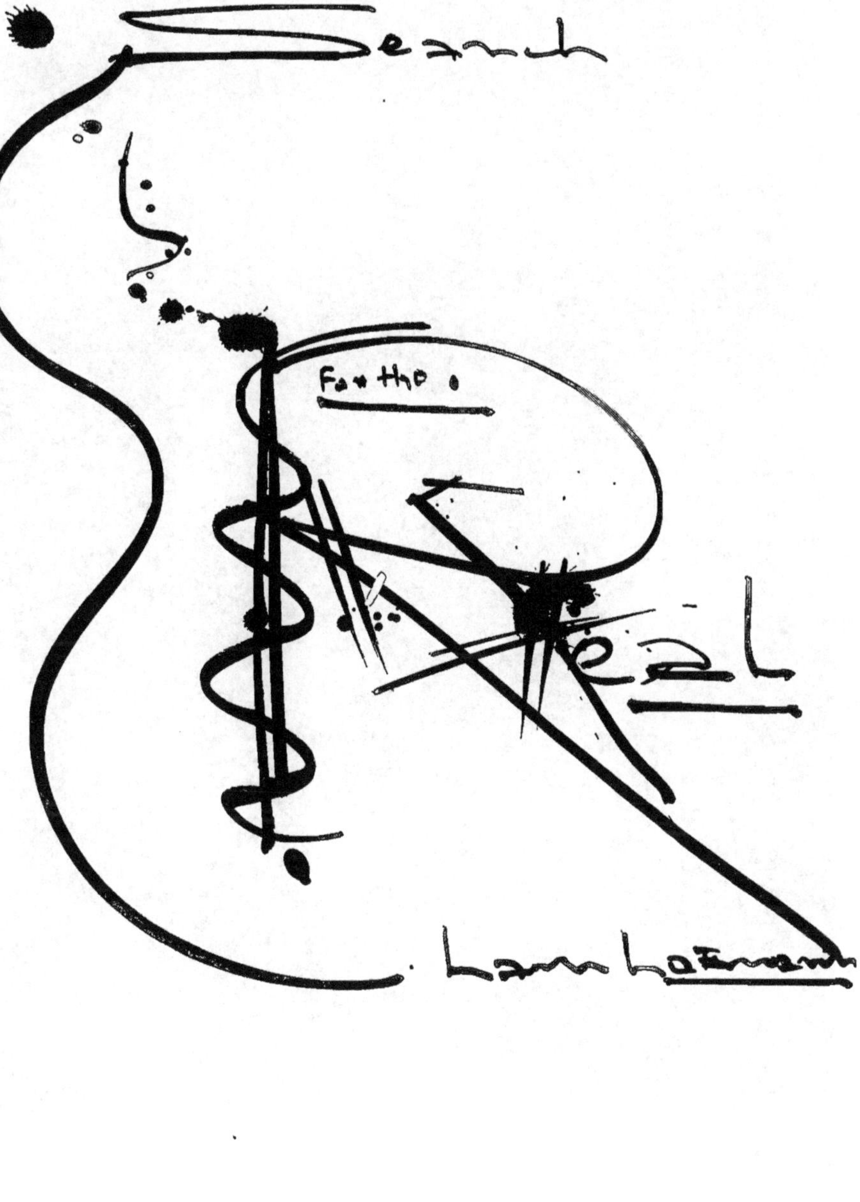
Search
For the
Real
Hans Hofmann

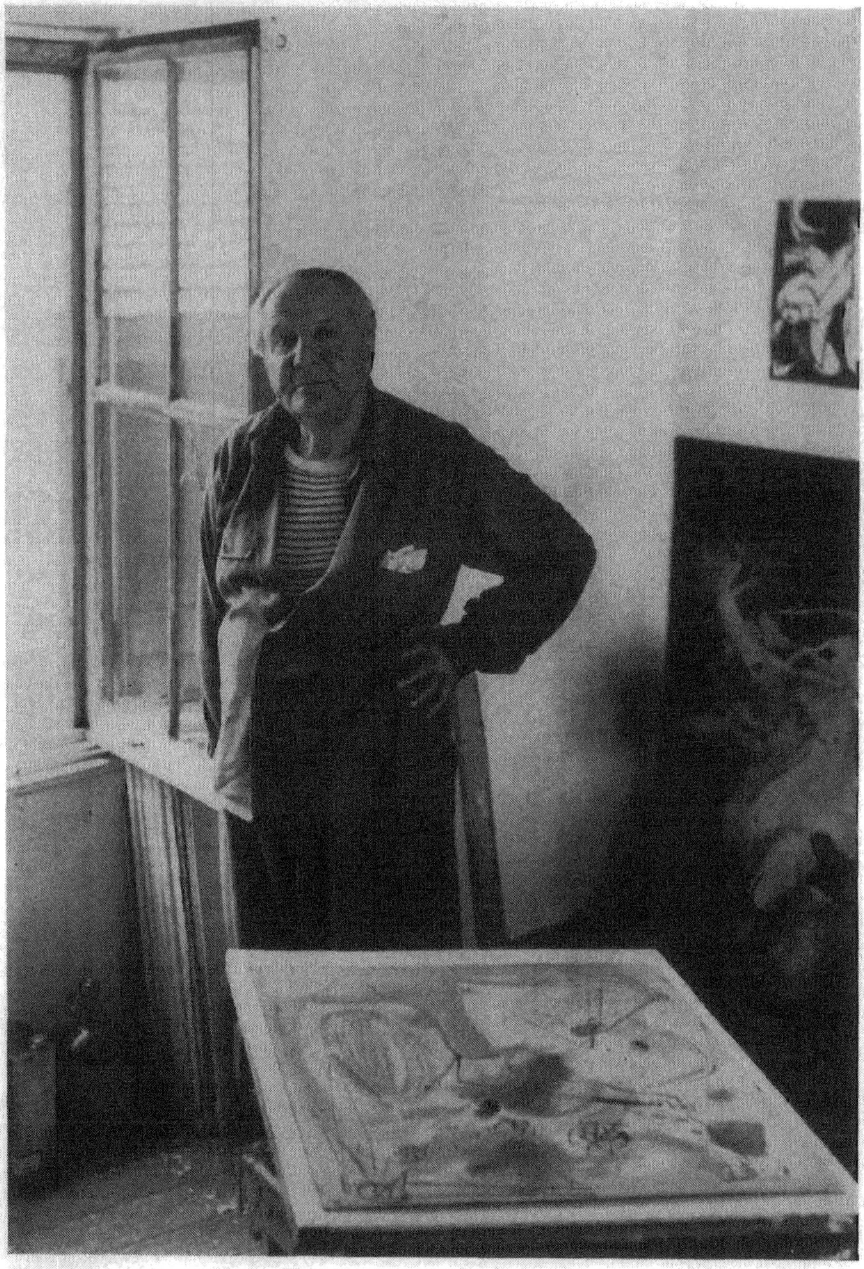

Hans Hofmann, 1948

Contents

HANS HOFMANN, 1948	Frontispiece
ACKNOWLEDGMENTS	6
INTRODUCTION by Bartlett H. Hayes, Jr.	7
TABLE OF EXHIBITIONS	16
ILLUSTRATED INTRODUCTION—Illustrations marked * are reproduced in *Color Notes*	17
THE SEARCH FOR THE REAL IN THE VISUAL ARTS	46
SCULPTURE	55
PAINTING AND CULTURE	60
EXCERPTS FROM THE TEACHING OF HANS HOFMANN—Adapted from the essays *On the Aims of Art* and *Plastic Creation*	65
TERMS	76

APPENDIX:

Visual catalogue of the Retrospective exhibit of Hans Hofmann at the Addison Gallery, 1948	80
Color Notes	91

Acknowledgments

In presenting this explanation of abstract art, as represented in the painting and writing of Hans Hofmann, the Addison Gallery acknowledges gratefully the following assistance:

To Miss Betty Parsons, Mr. Samuel M. Kootz, Miss Lenita Manry, Miss Sue Mitchell, Miss Alice Hodges, Miss Lilian O'Linsey, Mr. and Mrs. Patrick Morgan, for their helpful advice in assembling the exhibition from which this volume has grown;

To Miss Mercedes Carles, Mr. Ludwig Sander, Mr. Ernst Stoltz, Mr. Glen Wessels, for translations of various writings;

To the Editors of *The Fortnightly*, periodical, San Francisco, and the Editors of *The League*, magazine of The Art Students League, New York, in which some of these writings originally appeared;

To Mr. Maurice Berezov, for photographs of Mr. and Mrs. Hofmann; to Mr. Wilfried Zogbaum and Mr. Bill Witt respectively for frontispiece and tailpiece;

To Miss Perle Fine, Mr. Fred Hauck, Mr. George McNeil, ass't professor, University of Wyoming, and Professor Worth Ryder, University of California, for helpful evaluation of the teaching of Hans Hofmann;

Above all, to Miz Hofmann, who, with her husband, has helped with editorial sifting and rendered authentically vital what might otherwise have been merely academically speculative.

Introduction

Curving slowly through the fertile farmland of Central Bavaria, the Altmuehlthal barge canal skirts the grain fields which were once the economic substance of Frederik Manger, as well as the material substance of the best Munich beer. One proud March day in 1880, Herr Manger learned by the morning post that in the hamlet of Weissenburg, a few leagues away, his daughter had borne a son. Because the boy's father became a Government official shortly thereafter and moved his family to the more distant provincial capital, grandfather and grandson scarcely saw each other until several years had passed. Mutual affection was established, nevertheless, and, as he grew older, Hans Hofmann became a frequent visitor in his grandfather's wide fields, especially during the long summer days, when the city was hot and dusty.

The fields were hot, too, as the laborers worked to complete the first harvest, but the air was sweet smelling, and the cool water of the canal offered a place for a small boy to find welcome relief. It offered excitement as well. Young Hans would often be found perched on the bank watching the canal boats move slowly, endlessly, by. The canal was the busy link between the tributaries of the Rhine and the Danube and, in turn, between the ports of the North Sea and those of the Black Sea and the Mediterranean. What cargoes weighted these barges so deeply in the water? What strange sights might be found at the journey's end? The visions which the lad readily conjured up for his imagination seemed intimately associated with movement and the logical flow and counter-flow of this river traffic. Neither the North nor the South could have any meaning without the other, for wasn't their distant relationship the very essence of their trade? And the canal was the winding fluid line which related them.

But the canal furnished other interests. There were actually pictures to be found in it, animated pictures with shifting shapes which changed as the barges passed. Then, when the water stilled and became darkly serene, it was sometimes hard to tell where the canal left off and the fields began, so clear and motionless were the images. How clever of nature to reflect her own perfect likeness! But how deceitful, for, as the crack of a canal-man's whip and the bark of a river mongrel heralded the approach of another barge, the water would again become agitated and the images again altered. The nearer the barge would come, the more the green reflections would give way to silvery flashes of transparent ripples, and the more obviously would the canal appear to be what one had known it to be by actual experience... water. Was there a secret hidden in these shifting patterns of the canal surface? Was nature more truly to be revealed through perceiving its movements and its changing tensions than in the illusory impression brought to mind only through surface reflections?

The dinner-gong would occasionally ring in on his youthful speculations, and Hans would turn to watch the field-hands slowly threading their way through rows of ripening hops toward the farmhouse where his grandmother, empress of the household, had prepared a long table with the mid-day meal for all. Here was plenty, simple but wholesome; and as the conversation rose and fell, the migratory help came and went with the changing seasons. In the cyclical presence of these laborers, Hans observed anew the ceaseless flux of nature, now dynamic, now static, changing forever, yet always on the point of change. Strangers became friends, and friends soon moved on; but the pattern remained the same. Life as an abstract force was constant, but it could be experienced only through the balanced inconstancies of individual lives.

These were profound thoughts to be entertained by one so young, and it is possible that their meaning was but half realized by the boy at that time. Yet if he failed to sense fully the importance of his musings, his father appreciated them even less. Hans was bundled off to school, where a creditable performance in science and mathematics partially restored parental approval. However, the methodical family life of a provincial official could offer but a stern future to a young dreamer who opposed the hum of domestic routine with the treble of his violin and the resonant vibrations of the organ. Fortified with an abstract but positive feeling for relationships of interval and tone, he soon transferred his musical concepts to painting and to pictorial problems which paralleled his musical experience. These problems were to become an unending series: a continuing process of formulating ever new evaluations. They were to preempt his energies all the rest of his life. His search for the real had begun.

The search actually began in a practical way when the incipient break with his father finally came to a climax, and, as a young man of sixteen, he set forth, resolved to make his own way. Artistic independence was not to be readily achieved, however, especially by one whose immature drawings were but grudging barter for food. To obtain funds for study, he was, therefore, obliged to carry the search into unexpected corners.

In one of those corners, he found a harvest of knowledge upon which he satiated his appetite for mechanics. Through the influence of his father, he had obtained work as a youthful assistant to the Director of Public Works of the State of Bavaria. He spent hours among the shelves of the Engineering Library, absorbing technical information which finally resulted in his inventing an electromagnetic comptometer, (somewhat similar to the now familiar calculating machine). Patent papers were signed by his mother for he was not yet of legal age. He would not allow his father to assist. The latter watched the progress of the prodigy with satisfaction, nevertheless. Late one afternoon, a mutual friend visited the young inventor. "Your father wishes me to tell you that you have done well," he said. "He hopes that you will find this useful." The visitor then poured a stream of gold upon the desk. A thousand marks! Here was pay for his mechanic, and more, much more for new equipment!

That night was not for sleep. The glittering coins struck a spark which kindled the inflammable store of his daydreams. Now he would set himself to developing other contrivances, and his resources would increase. He would have many things...a house, a well-equipped laboratory, a horse and carriage — well, just a horse, perhaps, to ride in the early mornings when nature always appeared most vigorous. Life was better when it was vigorous and sure; too often it was weak and uncertain, and then one was always faced with the problem of reconciling the two extremes. Visions of affluence crowded upon him in swift sequence until, like the enchanted palaces of children's tales, they were dispelled at cockcrow by the practicalities of the coming day.

He rose and went out. The air of early autumn was bracing, like the air of the mountains. It seemed firm and real, almost as if he might hold it in his hands. It was strange, he thought, how reality is so often associated with the sense of touch. Surely there were other qualities as real as the solidness of things! A rapid turn along the Isar recalled memories of the gentle canal, only here the water flowed powerfully, and, as the sun mounted above the treetops and went higher into the sky, the river became a torrent of gold, and then, with the advance of day, more realistically silver. The whole world, like the river, was so mighty, yet so mutable! What single aspect of it could present this contrast? An artist would have to make many adjustments even to attempt it.

A flock of wild duck floated rapidly by toward the Isar bridge. He watched them bob about on the surface until they were all but lost to view against the monumental foaming ruffs which encircled the piers. Suddenly, as if by an agreed signal, they rose all at once and restored a sense of pictorial equilibrium by flying upstream to the bend in the river whence they had started. There they settled and enacted their picturesque role all over again. Movement and counter-movement; it was the very lifeblood of nature.

Now he was back again in the city which was already stirring. More and more people came out into the cobbled streets. As the morning wore on, shadows were flattened against the walls, crowded aside by the turbulent brilliance of urban life. So dynamic was the scene that it appeared all at once to be totally immobile. Each element was completely in balance with every other, yet, like the itinerant laborers on his grandfather's farm, the crowd shifted irregularly within itself. How unlike the precisely monotonous, always predictable movements of a machine! Perhaps one should strive to pin down this air of vitality whereby order emerged from disorder. If he could convert it into paint, preserve without possibility of change the feeling of vibrant movement, might he not discover laws hitherto unperceived?

He turned into the Theatinerstrasse, the wide thoroughfare of the business center, and walked quickly past richly filled shop windows where each article was ticketed with a fragment of his daydreams. Continuing straight on to the bank, he deposited the money his father had sent him. He then performed two errands which advanced him far along the way of his search — he registered at Art School and got married.

These were the years which furnished the basic experience shared alike by all art students: work, some play, more work, discouragement and renewed faith, trial and error, awe of the Master alternating with a barely contained patience of him when some youthful sortie into the realm of experiment was curtly rebuffed because all the arts must be ruled by discipline and discipline is the noble art of following the rules and minding the task at hand. One must know the landmarks if he is to have freedom of movement; else he is lost.

A succession of masters whose names were destined to disappear in the mediocrity of their traditional outlook — Michailow, Aspe, Ferenczi, Grimwald — helped him learn his basic lessons well. These lessons were to be the foundation-stone of his later teaching, as well as his own work. First, the stone must be shaped, as well as placed; and so he learned that rules vary with experience, as customs vary with the climate. This, it seemed, was the most fundamental rule of all.

His scientific faculties proved to be an asset in the concentrated analysis of artistic problems. Science helped him survey nature broadly and objectively and supplied the material for further creative speculation. He was naturally curious, and his initial success encouraged him to venture further. A shipwreck, much dramatized in the news of 1898, inspired experiments with high frequency radiation and resulted in a submarine signal-device to warn vessels of unseen dangers at sea. Other inventions followed. Sensitizing an electric bulb by exposing it to extremely high potentials, produced a light, he found, which, if it did not show brightly, at least glowed continuously, independent of an electric source. It would be a boon to the coal miner, perhaps, if it could be improved and developed commercially, but, more absorbed with ideas than merchandizing, he abandoned this experiment to contrive a portable freezing unit for preserving food on maneuvers. Not everyone, he realized, was able to live in the generous circumstances his grandmother had provided. This utilitarian device might be of service.

That there were no profits from all this activity was of small concern. Had he been less inept at business, he might have become launched on a successful scientific career, and his search for artistic verity might have ceased. Instead, these explorations were but instruments to help him plot his aesthetic course. It was becoming apparent to him that he must seek reality within the principles which guide human experience. The normally observed arrangements of weights and measurements, planes, textures and colors were no more than the material evidence of those principles.

About this time he became acquainted with Willi Schwarz, a repatriated artist who had brought theories from Paris which were then unknown to Hofmann's former teachers. "One must observe nature by means of the light reflected from objects, rather than be concerned with the tangible existence of the objects themselves." How provocative! Yet how limiting to his search for inner truth! There must be some way of bringing about a transformation of optical experiences in order to reveal a direct relation between nature and the mind — some way to create an expression of both through the medium of the picture.

Willi was profoundly impressed with Hofmann's versatility and intellectual capacity and effected a meeting between his new friend and the nephew of a Berlin collector. The latter introduced him, in turn, to his wealthy uncle, Philip Freudenberg. And so it came about that one wintry morning in 1904 the aspiring artist looked out of the railway carriage window at the Gare de l'Est in Paris — looked out a little bewildered, but not a bit abashed, at a new world — a world which was to be increasingly his during the decade to come. He had a patron, a friend with faith in him. The realization made him step confidently to the platform and, after assisting his wife to alight, stride through the usual bustle of the station throng. He smiled uncomprehendingly at the rapid chatter of the porters and carried his luggage himself. He had always acted independently; why should he seek help in this minor matter?

Proceeding toward their destination, the pair paused at a café near the summit of Montparnasse to warm chill fingers with a sip of hot coffee. Suddenly they realized they were hungry after the long journey and in hesitant French, which was reinforced with the positive gestures of sign language, he asked for bread. As the waiter disappeared, they sat back to contemplate the surroundings. These were not like the oak-beamed halls of Munich, neither were they wholly strange. They were unfamiliar rather than fundamentally different. But not so with the language. Although simple phrases were adequate for essential needs, here was a barrier to ideas as well as a channel for them. One became so accustomed to linguistic habits it was difficult to learn new ones. The more habits one had, the more limited one grew. Habits must be avoided then. Only habits which are basic for all things are to be tolerated, and even these with suspicion, for what is basic can only be assumed, never known with certainty. If one is to progress, one must be ever alert, ever changing. In painting, this could be so too — even in painting.

The waiter returned and placed some croissants before them. What kind of bread was this? Never before had humble grain achieved such a metamorphosis! They must remember this place and find it again. He paid the check, tucked his portfolio under his arm, and, as they went out, turned to look at the sign over the door. It was simple to remember, Café du Dôme.

Needless to say, they retraced their steps to the Café for it soon became the favored haunt of the forward looking artists and writers of the day. Passionate discussions, as well as gaiety, ruled the impromptu gatherings. Radical theories were ardently opposed one to the other, yet all were tolerated, for art can flourish in no other atmosphere. Perhaps the validity as well as the vitality of ideas nurtured on such occasions depended to no small degree on their joint catholicity. Though the disputants represented many nationalities, their common belief in the spiritual necessity of the arts was international. There were the Frenchmen, Braque, Delaunay and Matisse; the Spaniards, Picasso and Gris; the Norwegians, Munk and Karsten; the Bulgar, Pascin; the American, Carles; and many others who were habitués besides Hofmann and his fellow countrymen. Hofmann himself had now been honored with a show in Berlin, and had exhibited there besides, with the *Neue Secession*. Among these friends in Paris, most of whom were as yet little known to the public at large, his prestige was assured.

Although his interest in Science never totally died away during these broadening years, it persisted more as a philosophic index for his aesthetic experiments than as a seriously protracted pursuit. Not that household devices were not handily improvised as the need warranted, but there was a difference between constructing and operating simple utilitarian objects and comprehending the scientific theories which they represented in such a small way. That was the trouble with the modern world: so many people had learned to control machines who knew nothing of the principles by which they operated and who were as ready to abuse as to use what they didn't fully understand. Indeed, the shape of the entire social order was being reworked in the mold of scientific discovery. Yet only a handful of artists seemed to be in the least aware of the resultant implications, and their concern aroused but derisive outcries from a scornful public. He must think more about this. Surely, there should be a way to paint ideas of such import rather than confine one's attention merely to the outward manifestations of this vital self-generated change!

And now, as he sought more deeply the illusive realities which motivate life, the world itself was changed. It happened that in the summer of 1914,

Hofmann was forced to forsake the liberality of Paris, leaving behind him the bulk of his labor. It was never to be retrieved.

To let go one's past is, in a sense, to lose one's way. And to lose one's way requires a moment's pause, at least, in order to find oneself again. The duration of that moment cannot be measured by any common unit of time, for experience possesses a value more enduring than time. It was to be expected, therefore, that after the frenzied dash homeward, Hofmann would take breath, and then survey the aesthetic ground.

Throughout the first years of the war, Munich was relatively unharried. The Kaiser's armies had swept on with power and confidence and, although an occasional citizen might inwardly deplore their cause, it was treason even to disapprove. One was, perforce, led to acquiesce. There was an opportunity to carry on extraordinary, as well as ordinary, affairs; and so in 1915 Hofmann took stock of his altered circumstances and established, in the city where he had received his academic training, a school for modern art.

His reasons for undertaking the venture at this time were partly practical, partly idealistic; he needed money as much as he needed confidence. He also felt that the materialistic views entertained by the public generally could never improve the chaotic conditions prevailing the world over. Only by facing these conditions on emotional, as well as intellectual, levels could they be properly sensed and analyzed. Art, primarily concerned with creating visual order, provided a means whereby one might feel one's way emotionally into the nature of such problems. An artist could at least seek to abstract aesthetic and spiritual values and make them visible in preference to producing purely descriptive illustrations of physical objects. If it were commonly understood, modern art might even become a cultural force for restoring an emotional stability to society. Thus, the school, in the suburb of Schwabing, became the pulpit from which Hofmann preached the creed he had helped formulate, the creed he had brought with him, his sole possession, from Paris.

Months dragged on; then the tide of battle turned. The routine of living became harder and harder to manage. Supplies grew short, and in the face of every-day needs it became difficult to convince his dwindling class that anything could be more important than the mere business of maintaining an existence.

One afternoon in the fall of 1918, he began to wonder if he shouldn't abandon the crusade. His energies had been exhausted while promoting the welfare of others. His own work had suffered. His teaching was now a chore instead of a stimulus. He argued with himself a long time, standing by the window as darkness came on. He watched the brightening stars, now one, then another, then several more. Each new star changed the pattern ever so slightly, for, as it appeared all the rest moved over, as if by common consent, to readjust themselves in his vision and make room for the new. This organizing and reorganizing of twinkling points of light seemed much like painting. Just as in vision, each planet was in actual tension with every other in the system — in relative tension that caused it to swing in an unseen orbit, obeying unseen laws, even into translucent infinity. If one looked long enough, these relationships and hidden forces appeared even more real than the array of the stars themselves. The difficulty with material things on earth was that they were generally too close and too familiar to be readily sensed according to their true related significance. Of course, painters could, if properly trained, make allowances for false impressions of vision. Yes; it would be right to continue the school, to continue it at all costs.

He lowered his eyes to the city. Suddenly, flashes of fire showed beyond the housetops, as if flowers had fallen from the firmament. What strange stars were these? The fireworks continued to celebrate for several hours. The anguished years of war had ended.

Time seemed to have stopped during the next few weeks. Even nature herself paused in the warm memory of summer, ignoring winter's inevitable coming. It was enough just to be conscious of being, to walk unhurriedly about, to make doubly sure that familiar corners had not been destroyed, to know that normal life could be resumed. Students now appeared at the school in greater, ever greater, numbers. There was little time to dally.

So life moved forward. Each step ahead lent confidence for the next advance. Progress was nearly erased by the sudden Revolution of 1921 which, nevertheless, was over almost before it began and, like the streetcars which continued their droning schedule despite bursts of machine gun fire from all sides, the school maintained daily operation. Indeed, it could not stop. The human business at hand was more vital than man's greedy brawling with his fellow man.

The fame of Number Forty Georgenstrasse carried far in these postwar years. Soon students came from abroad — perhaps to learn what was too obvious to be taught by the traditional methods of schooling at home; perhaps because they were restless, anxious to assume new conveniences for old, new fashions for the worn, yet tediously slow to replace outmoded beliefs or change cumbersome customs; perhaps, somehow, because new ideas needed to be officially approved before they could be confessed. Brought back from other lands, these ideas might become endowed with respectability out of regard for their very foreignness. Whatever the reason, fame resulted in summer schools away from Munich, in the nearby mountains that divide Bavaria and Austria, then at Ragusa, again at Capri, next at St. Tropez.

Now his students experienced the difficulty with language which Hofmann himself had encountered long ago in Paris. Because of the abstract nature of words, it was always hard to differentiate the multiple shades of meaning or to utter one's thoughts with clarity; yet to understand the plastic significance of painting was truly still more difficult, even for practising painters. So often people believed themselves able to grasp at a glance what actually required experience and empathy to be realized fully. Rather than blaming themselves, they blamed the object which baffled their comprehension. It took patience to teach, therefore, that recognition of objects is not a determinant for evaluating art; that aesthetic meaning results only from perceiving relationships whether consciously or not; that art, like language and science, is understandable only to those who develop the insight to understand it.

Accustomed to interspersing his summer expeditions with frequent trips to Paris, returning seasonally to the frost-feathered winters of Munich, Hofmann one day found himself gazing out at the undulating Atlantic in a mixed mood of uncertainty and anticipation. This time, he was alone. He had been summoned to teach at the University of California. The year was 1930. Two years later he was to settle permanently on these shores.

However, this was farthest from his thoughts as he watched mounds of water jousting in a tempestuous oceanic tournament. The ship advanced through the arena opposing confusion with purpose, its yawing spray-drenched deck appearing expressively resolute in relation to the horizonless tumult about it. It was hard to believe that this was the same boat which, a few days before, had dispassionately furrowed the soundless unmoving surface. He realized anew that the expression of mood in nature, as in art, arises from a state of vibrant inter-relationships, not from the simple independent being of static objects. Pondering in this fashion, he pulled a small notebook from his pocket, shielded it from the distracting wind with a corner of his cape, and began to explore his observations with the probing lines of his pencil. Form and counterform, involution and evolution, the reason for abstract drawing was to fix abstract concepts so that their fleeting presence would not escape contemplation; but one must take care to avoid a cataleptic image of material nature which could no more express these concepts than could the actual objects themselves if all things were to be stilled.

The more his pencil traced the voids and volumes of the sea, the more he saw that what he had mistaken for confusion was actually a vigorous representation of order on an enormous scale. He had been too intent on the superficial appearance of the scene to note it properly. With study he perceived how the unseen force of the wind whipped the waves into intervals controlled by the physical nature of the water. To reproduce the appearance of the wave was merely to show the effect of the force, not to portray it. As he continued to draw the inter-penetrating action of the elements, he discovered that even the fluid change of form was subject to its own laws, just as was the evolution of shapes which originated in the organic and geometric character of solid things. Nature was basically an equation ready to be resolved by the scientist and by the sensitive artist as well.

He thought of this again a few days later as the vessel steamed slowly toward the imposing prospect of New York City. America loomed mightily before him — a country which, in spite of its gossamer structures and prismatic cities, scarcely yet knew its aesthetic strength. But with all its energy it would learn, learn by the searching growth of its work, as a painting grows in the plastic process, or a truth emerges from the trials of the laboratory. Perhaps, in his own way, he might be able to help a little.

* * * * *

1930 — Instructor at University of California (summer)
1931 — Instructor at University of California (summer)
1931 — Instructor at Chouinard Art Institute (summer)
1932–1933 — Instructor at Art Students League (winter)
1933 — Instructor at Thurn School, Gloucester (summer)
1934 — Instructor at Thurn School, Gloucester (summer)
1934 — Founded Hofmann School of Art, New York
1935 — Founded Hofmann School of Art, Provincetown

Hans Hofmann Exhibitions:

Neue Secession, Berlin, 1909
Paul Cassirer, Berlin, 1910
California Palace of the Legion of Honor, San Francisco, 1931
Isaac Delgado Museum, New Orleans, 1941
Art of This Century, New York, 1944
The Arts Club of Chicago, 1944
67 Gallery, New York, 1945
Betty Parsons Gallery, New York, 1946, 1947
Samuel Kootz Gallery, New York, 1947
Addison Gallery of American Art, Andover, 1948
Gallerie Maeght, Paris, 1949

STUDENT DRAWING 1898
Pencil   8¾" x 10⅝"

These drawings were made by Hofmann while he was a student in the school of Moritz Heymann, at Munich, 1898. Hofmann's early interest in the creative contrast of line against line, form against form is apparent in the accented curves (below, left), and in the definition of volume by means of abrupt dark and light planes (below).

STUDENT DRAWING 1898
Pencil   8" x 11½"

STUDENT DRAWING 1898
Pencil   8" x 11½"

PORTRAIT OF THE ARTIST'S WIFE   1901
Oil   27⅛" x 19⅛"

Hofmann's early paintings show that he passed through the same stages as many of his European and American contemporaries: School of Munich; Impressionist; Cubist; etc.

These two portraits are among the few surviving works Hofmann painted before coming to America in 1930. All the rest have been destroyed in the two world wars.

SELF-PORTRAIT*   1902
Oil   16⅛" x 19½"

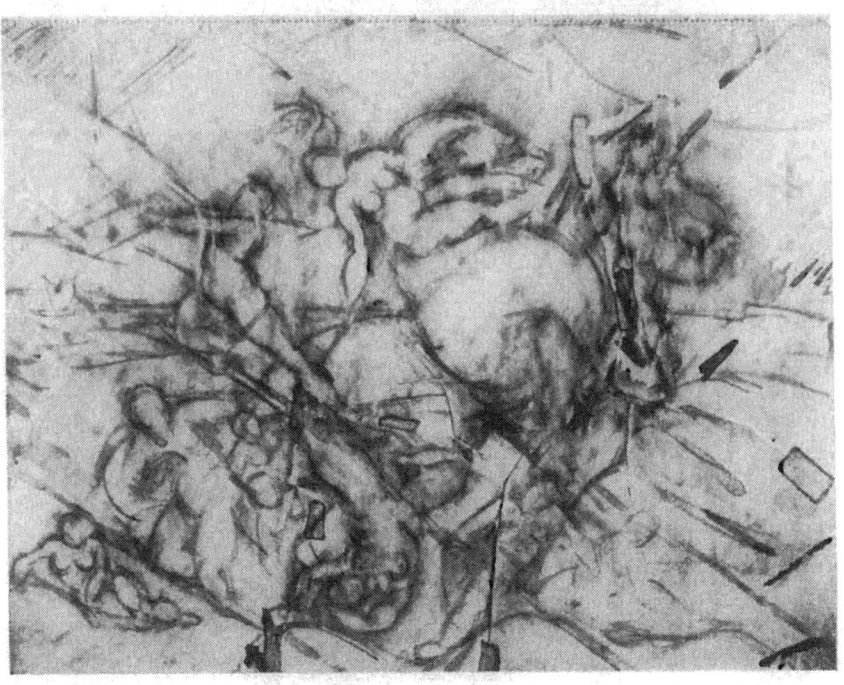

CEILING DESIGN   1914
Pencil-Watercolor-Collage   8⅛" x 10¼"

This drawing is a colored sketch for a ceiling decoration. The figures have been cut out and recomposed—a process which anticipates Hofmann's later preocupation with *relationships*. The ability to secure "an internal order existing between objects rather than stress their separate identities" is for him the key to the search for meaning amid the complexities of modern experience. What, in his later abstract painting, might be mistaken for casual pattern is actually this search made visible. It has its roots in these early studies.

GREEN BOTTLE   1921
Oil   16⅝" x 22⅞"

Form and color and the two-dimensional flatness of the picture surface begin to be more important pictorially than the representation of objects.

APPLES   1931   *Collection of Miss Alice Hodges*
Oil   25" x 30"   *Miss Lilian O'linsey*

St. Tropez 1927-28
Ink 10⅝" x 13⅝"

In Europe Hofmann's chief problem in regard to landscape was one of simplifying and grouping a number of unrelated forms and of creating within them an infinite variation of interrelated surface forms and textures.

California Oil Fields 1930
Ink 8½" x 10⅞"

When he arrived in California in 1930, the industrial activity and the vast expanse of the country made an overwhelming impression on Hofmann. To be realized and fully absorbed, these fresh experiences had to be drawn directly. Having finally become familiar with the new environment, he was free to simplify and select; once again the organization of space and form dominated his interest.

Trees and Landscape, California 1931
Ink 8½" x 10⅞"

ISLAND IN THE BAY, CALIFORNIA   1931
Ink   10⅝" x 13⅝"

In Hofmann's simplified representations of landscape, such as the drawing above, it is possible to observe shapes which reappear in his later abstract paintings as fully developed compositions.

"A work of Art goes through many phases of development, but in each phase it is always a work of art. Therein lies the importance of sketches."

RECLINING NUDE   1928
Ink   10⅝" x 13⅝"

Hofmann's figure drawings illustrate a progression, similar to the landscape series, from early studies of naturalistic shapes to a powerful development of planes and volumes in space. However, his work does not always evince the orderly sequence suggested by these and other illustrations in this volume. New experiments are gropingly encountered; they are seldom consciously planned. Old mannerisms frequently follow new inventions. Each advance is tested; each backward look is made with a surety which arises only from familiarity. Though generally chronological, much of the work must be dated approximately. From among the numerous portfolios and several thousand drawings, Hofmann himself cannot assign a precise moment to any one. But dates are important only if they point a trend, and trends are significant only if they give meaning to what follows. Hofmann's quality as an artist may be observed in his logical, gradual, and often uncertainly dated evolution.

FIGURE DRAWING   1932-34
Ink   8⅜" x 10⅞'

FIGURE DRAWING 1932-34
Ink 8⅜" x 10⅞"

In Hofmann's earlier drawings dark areas represent planes turned from the light. They follow natural forms. Shadows occur in the nooks and crannies which are beneath and behind objects. They form essentially "realistic" patterns. The resulting composition is a copy of the arrangement of objects found in nature. (See drawings on facing page.) Later (lower drawing, this page), natural light sources are disregarded for the sake of imparting a pictorial vitality to the two-dimensional composition. The contrast of light and dark areas then becomes the coordinating element of the picture. Instead of being an imitative image of nature the picture now actually exists as a fresh experience.

FIGURE DRAWING 1932-34
Ink 10⅞" x 8⅜"

STUDENT WITH SPECTACLES   1926
Ink   13⅝" x 10⅝"

One of a series of portrait studies in which line, as the junction of two or more planes, is made to serve as a significant element in the composition. This structural use of line, as distinguished from representational outline, is particularly noticeable in the definition of the cheekbone, or the facets of the forehead. It foreshows the use of abstract linear components in certain of Hofmann's later work (opposite).

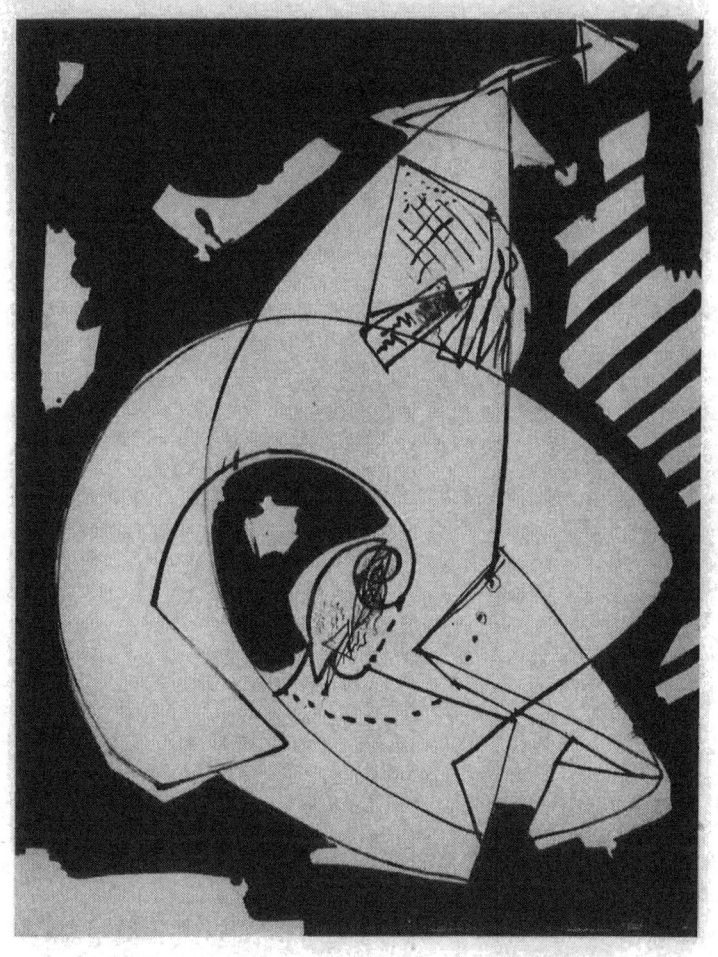

DRAWING 1945
Ink 41" x 30½"

Although graphic form received Hofmann's greatest attention in the years immediately following his arrival in America, color absorbed his interest after 1936. It became the agent which impelled him to experiment further with abstract composition for, not as closely associated as form with the description of recognizable objects, it allowed him greater freedom of invention.

Hofmann's use of color depended increasingly on seeking and defining relationships in space. Such external characteristics as local color and atmospheric effect gradually lost pictorial importance for him.

STILL LIFE, PINK TABLE*   1936
Casein   58¼" x 44½"

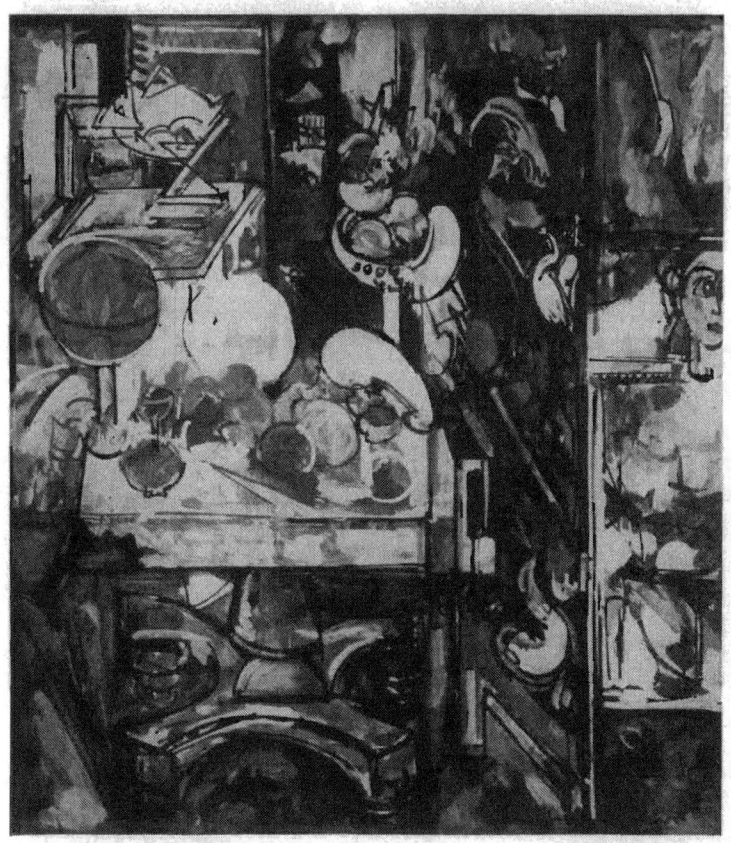

LITTLE BLUE INTERIOR*   1937-38
Oil   41⅜" x 35½"

The use of a single color (blue), which relates the floor-plane to the wall-plane, and the balance of strongly contrasted colors are examples of two plastic devices which are contrary to familiar 19th century forms of representation, but which are employed to affirm the two-dimensional nature of the picture (above). A picture is thus emphasized as an object to be evaluated and interpreted rather than to be misjudged as a substitute for the "real thing."

The pictorial devices noted above help compose diverse objects. The same devices also coordinate the many components of a single object (right).

STILL LIFE   1940
Wax Crayon and Ink
11¼" x 8¼"

An illusion of depth is obtained when objects are reflected by the two-dimensional surface of a normal mirror, but the images are related only by virtue of the objects they represent. By a plastic control of these reflected images, it is possible to emphasize the actuality of a painted surface, and by reorganizing the shapes achieve a pictorial unity not otherwise obtainable.

This "unnatural" process of creating pictorial order is, of course, a distortion of the usual experience of space, but it is no more illogical than the accepted literary practice of distorting the experience of time by arbitrarily rearranging the time sequence in a simple narrative, for the sake of constructing a unified dramatic truth.

STILL LIFE, MAGIC MIRROR   1939
Casein   50¼" x 35¼"

INTERIOR IN BLUE AND RED* 1941
Oil 44⅝" x 58¾"

31

The human figure embodies volumes and surface planes which are subject to plastic adjustment fully as much as in the case of inanimate objects.

The profile of a woman (right) is primarily a reorganization of natural volumes in terms of contrasting, flat color areas, but prepares the way for the architectural simplification of later work in which contraposed colors represent a fusion of solid forms with the space intervals which surround them (below and opposite).

SMALL PORTRAIT OF A WOMAN 1937-38
Oil 23¾" x 18½"

SELF PORTRAIT, THE KING* 1942
Oil 47½" x 42⅞"

SEATED WOMAN* 1944
Oil 70¾" x 60¾"

WHARVES (PROVINCETOWN)   1941
Wax Crayon and Ink   14" x 17"

From 1941 to 1943 innumerable landscape studies, executed with children's crayons, enabled Hofmann to resolve formal and spatial problems with those of color. In these drawings he frequently visualizes color as free standing, yet related, planes which define spatial intervals.

The role of color as an organizing and vitalizing element may be realized by comparing the illustrations opposite with the corresponding color notes on page 91.

PROVINCETOWN HARBOR   1941
Wax Crayon and Ink   11" x 14"

34

House On A Hill* 1941
Wax Crayon and Ink 14″ x 17″

A comparison of land and sky is an intellectual and abstract act on the part of the mind. Hofmann represents this act by balancing two or more areas of the same color which are visually brought together by lines connecting them (below).

Dunes And Sky* 1943
Watercolor 17½″ x 24″

The construction of this sun-flooded landscape is a logical synthesis of (a) the by-now-academic process, derived from the work of Cezanne, of building form through color, with (b) the integration of objective forms and spatial intervals for the sake of pictorial unity. In arriving at this stage of plastic independence, Hofmann seems to parallel aesthetically the outlook of modern scientific philosophers who conceive of the relative, interdependent existence of matter and space.

The yellow hue of sun and sand, the green bushes and the wavy contours of the dunes are still pictorially objective, however. Not until his plastic invention becomes subjective are the forms and colors wholly free. From here on, Hofmann's work is essentially a subjective visualisation of forces which are intuitively sensed beneath the surface appearance of nature. In common with artists of other times he now seeks a visual idiom to express some of the intangible aspects of experience. His work differs from theirs as much as experiences of the modern day differ from those of the past. It differs from that of his contemporaries to the extent that his personality and interpretive qualities likewise differ.

LANDSCAPE, "YELLOW SUN"*   1943
Oil   23⅝" x 29¾"

AGGRESSIVE 1944
Oil   30¾" x 41⅛"

Hofmann insists that, just as the poet and musician think in terms of words and sounds, the painter must think in terms of plane, line, form, space, and color. A relationship between any two of these, such as the tension between a white line and a black form, he calls a thought. The sum of such relationships he calls an idea. (See p. 46) Working with this approach, with the picture and the concept mutually influencing each other, he frequently has no title for a painting until he is done with it. Then for purposes of identification, he seeks one that will either recall his personal associations, or the final emotion of the work. Titles which appear on this and the following pages are no more than convenient tags and should not disconcert the reader.

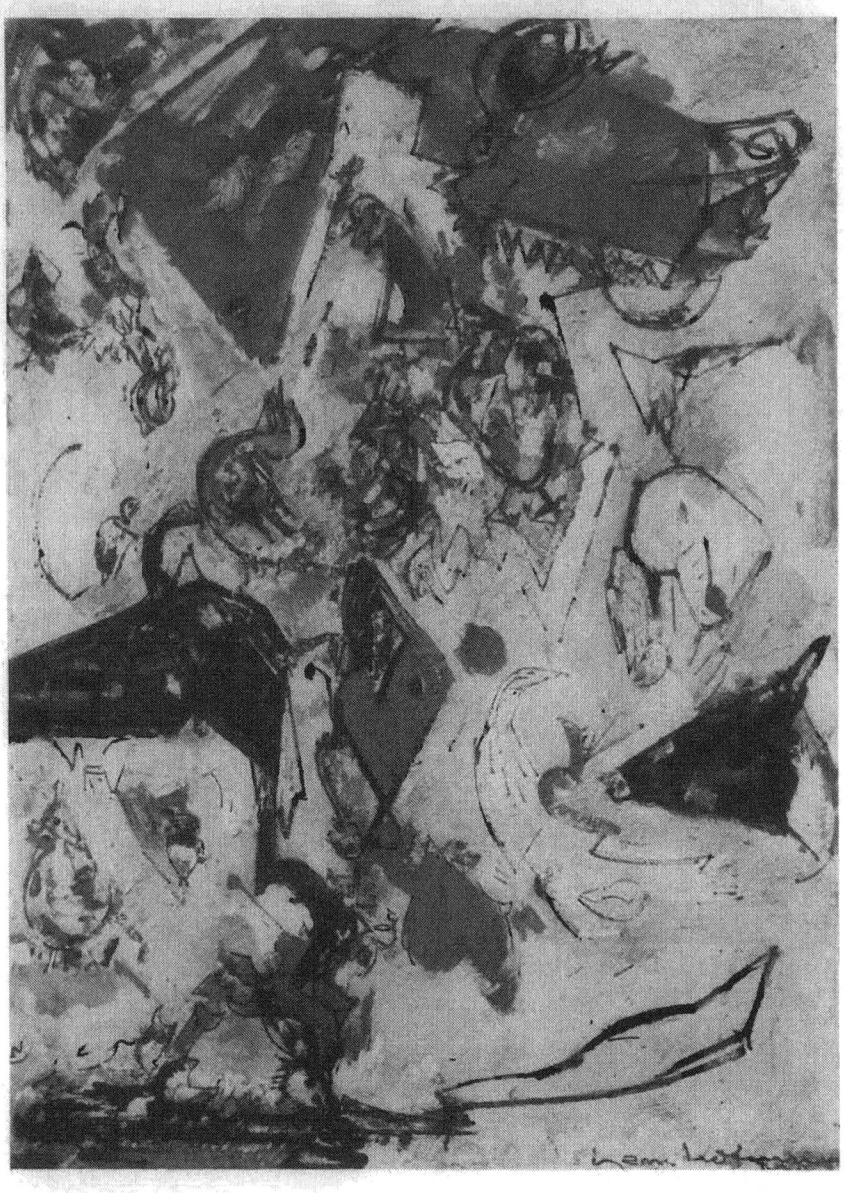

THE CIRCUS* 1945
Oil 55" x 40"

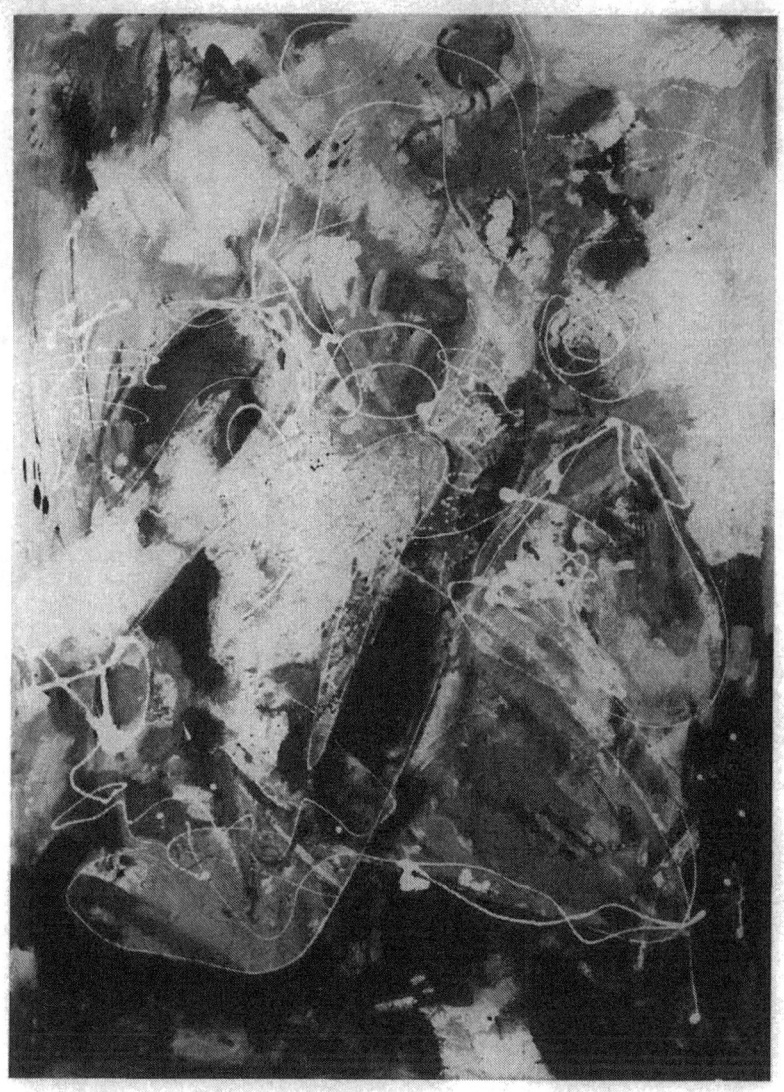

FANTASIA   1945-46
Mixed Technique   51⅛" x 35⅛"

The eye is quick to recognize a geometric arrangement, and, consequently, the relatively brittle, angular shapes of *The Circus* are apt to appear more controlled and thereby, perhaps, more purposeful than the "automatic" composition of *Fantasia*.

The universal search for abstract order does not consist solely in an alignment of material elements, however. These two pictures are contrasting examples of Hofmann's feeling for order: within objective nature on the one hand, and within the intuitive experiences of the spirit on the other.

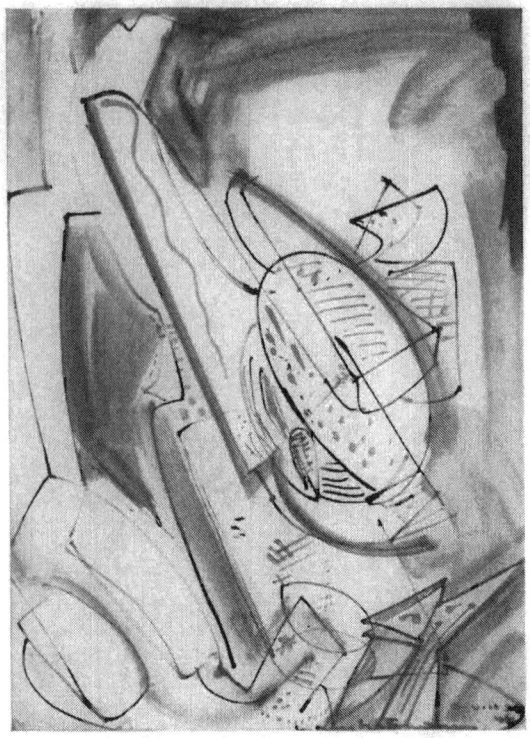

LIGHT FORMS 1946
Gouache 17½" x 23⅝"

In contrast to the wholly invented compositions of the two paintings on this page, the basic conditions of the picture opposite were previously established. Like Leonardo, who exercised his fancy upon the cracks and smudges of old plaster walls, Hofmann accepted the "visual premise" of an already paint-spattered surface and improvised upon it. This use of the accidental quality of the background no more invalidates the originality of the work, however, than the use of natural hillocks and ravines invalidates the creative discipline of the landscape architect. Philosophically, Hofmann thus recognizes the influence of environment on Man, yet knows that aesthetic meaning occurs only when an artist reveals his understanding of nature by recreating or altering it.

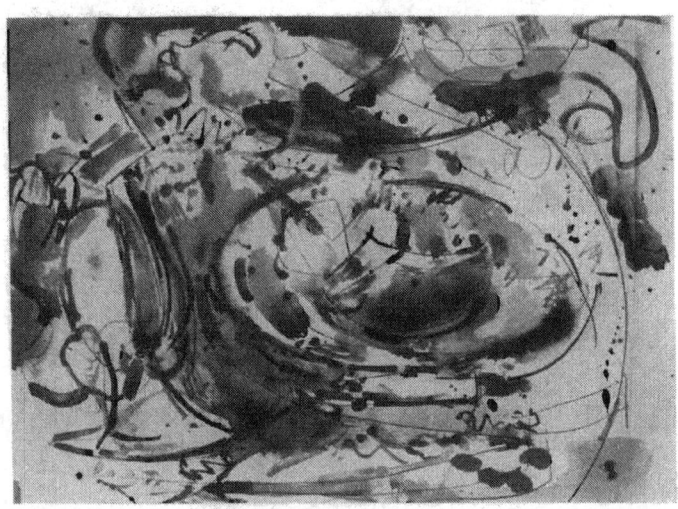

UNTITLED 1946
Watercolor 17½" x 23¾"

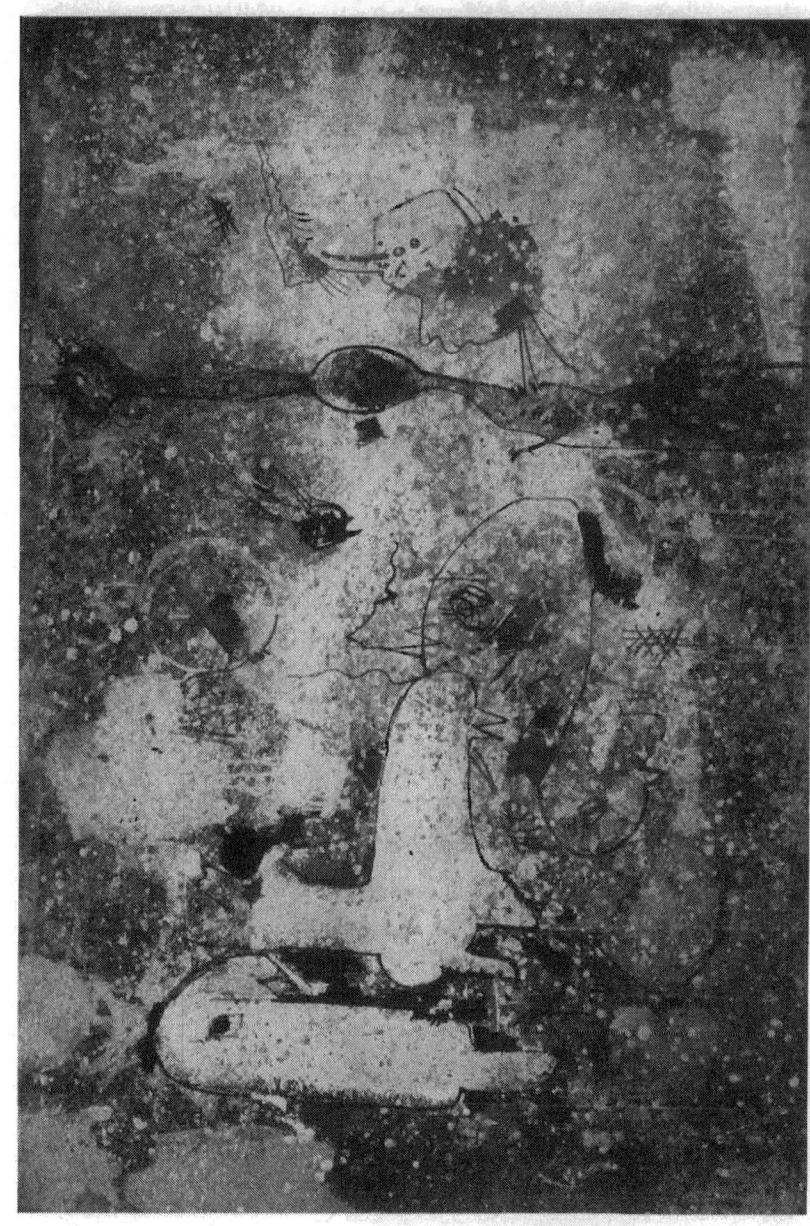

PALIMPSEST* 1947 39½" x 59½"
Oil and Gesso

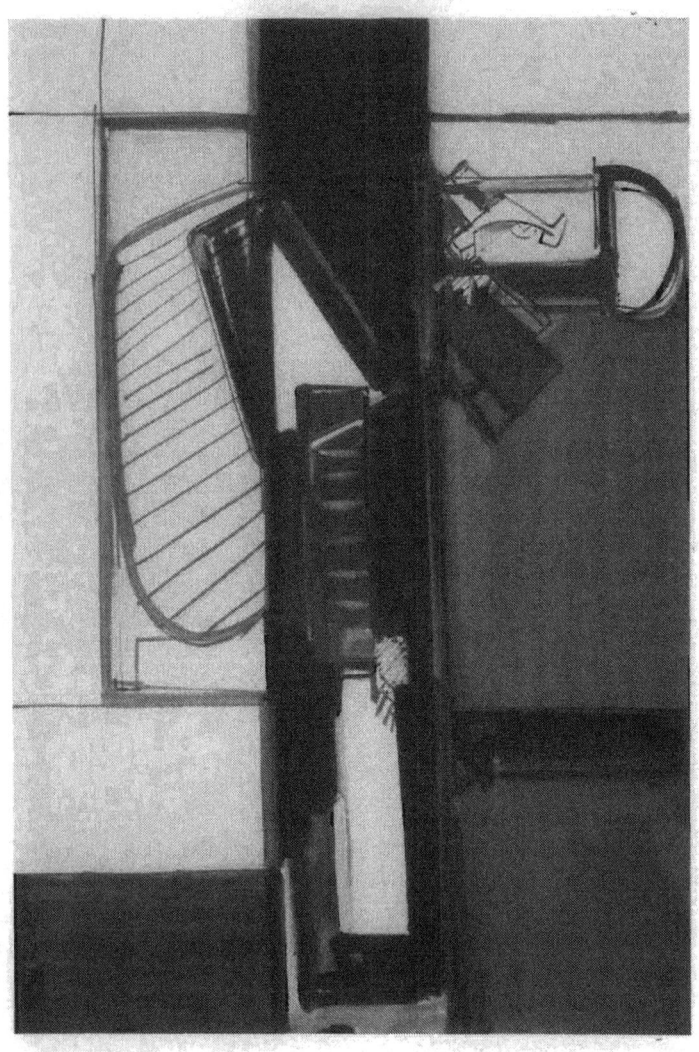

AWAKENING* 1947
Oil   60" x 40"

The variety of paintings produced during 1947 reveals something of Hofmann's inventive personality. His pictorial philosophy permits no crystallization of style, no formula. Attuned to the future, as well as to the present, each picture is nevertheless a synthesis of elements derived from precedent. In this flowering of plastic innovation upon the stalk of proven experience is his most significant contribution to modern aesthetics.

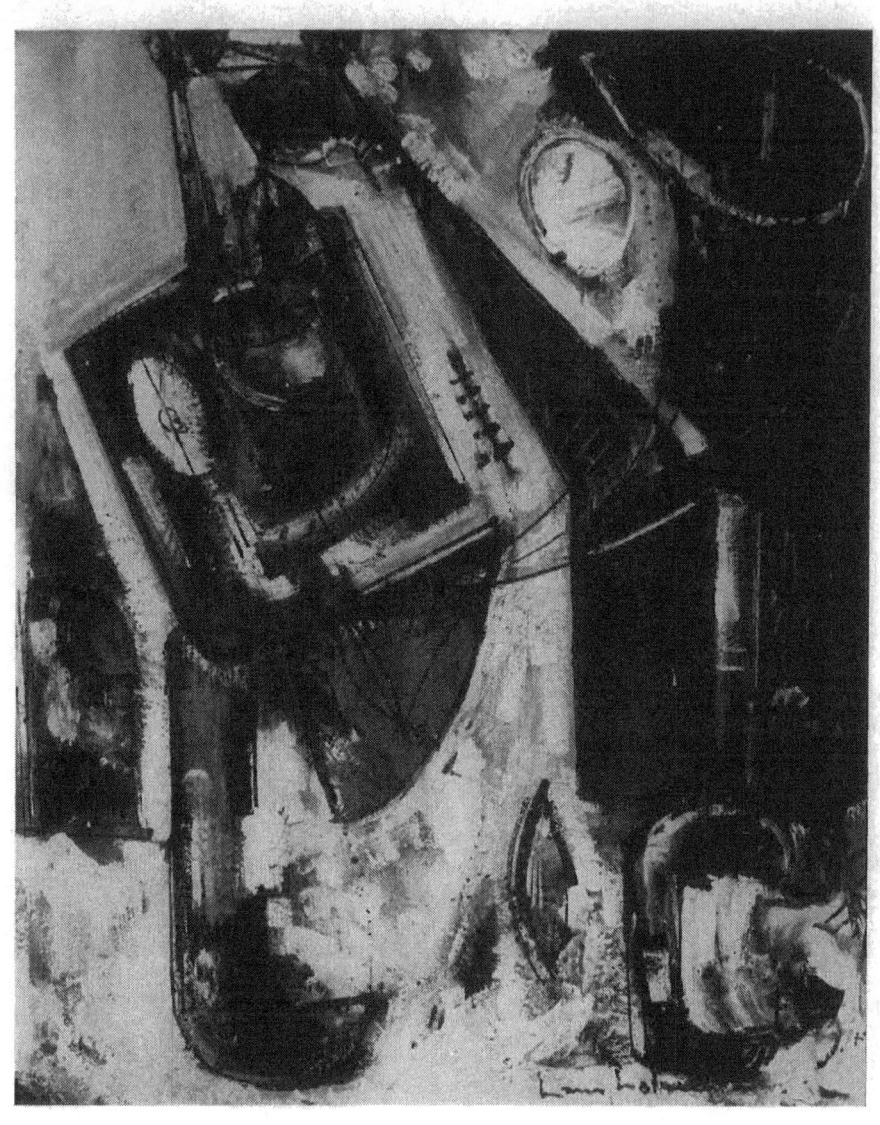

Delight* 1947
Oil 49¾" x 40"

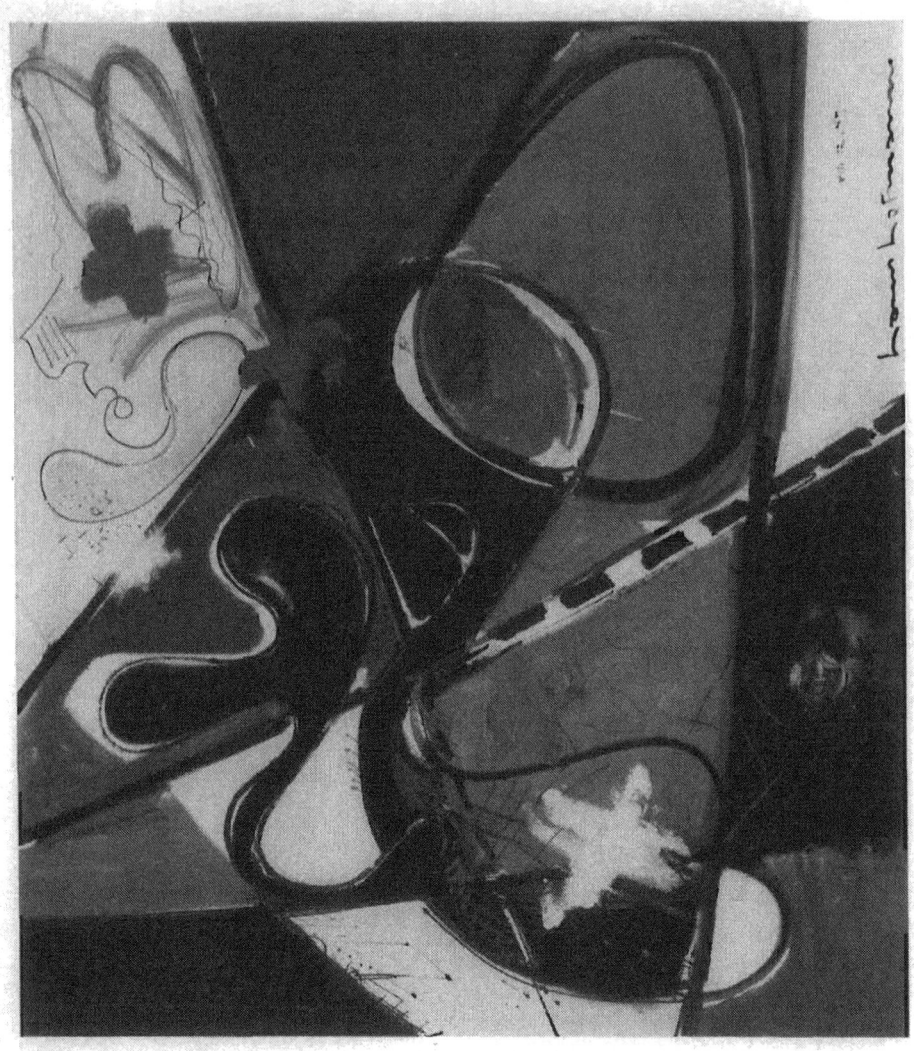

SUBMERGED 1947
Oil 60" x 68"

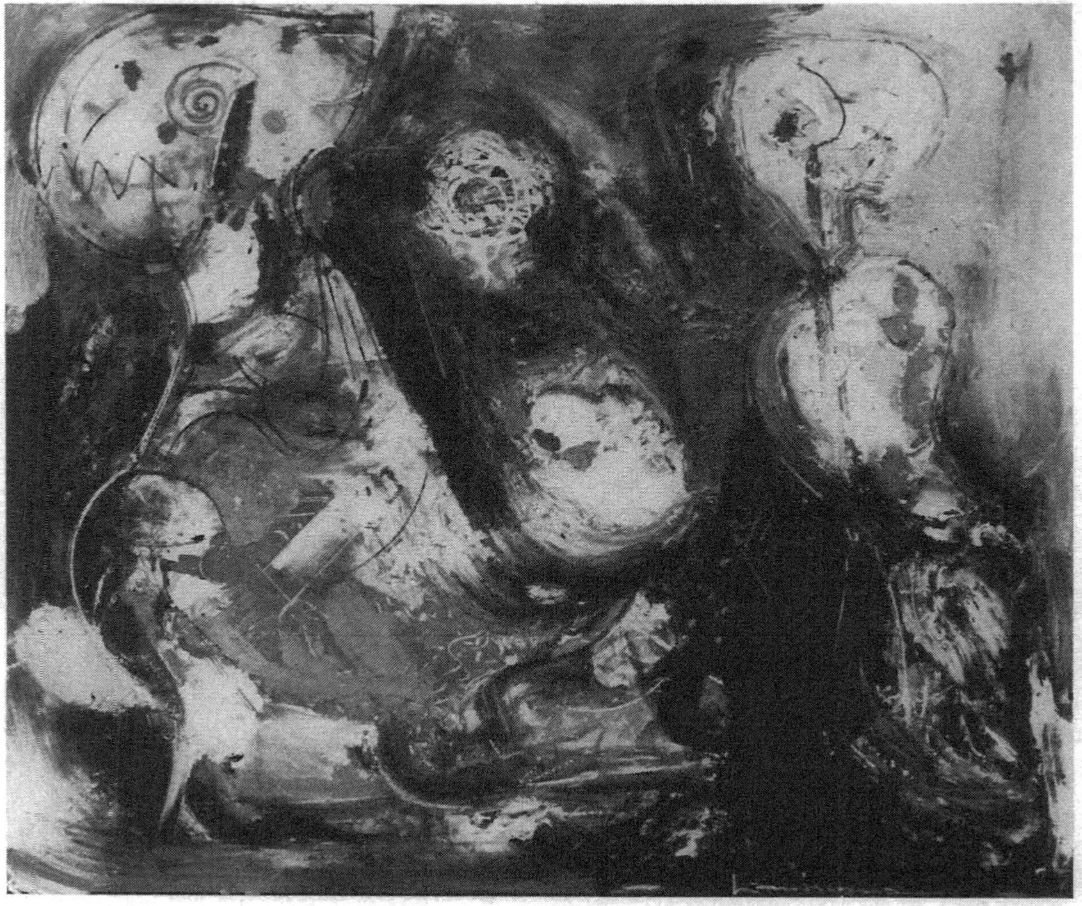

APPARITION* 1947
Oil 47½″ x 57⅜″

The Search for the *Real*
In the Visual Arts

Art is magic. So say the surrealists. But how is it magic? In its metaphysical development? Or does some final transformation culminate in a magic reality? In truth, the latter is impossible without the former. If creation is not magic, the outcome cannot be magic. To worship the product and ignore its development leads to dilettantism and reaction. Art cannot result from sophisticated, frivolous, or superficial effects.

The significance of a work of art is determined then by the quality of its growth. This involves intangible forces inherent in the process of development. Although these forces are surreal (that is, their nature is something beyond physical reality), they, nevertheless, depend on a physical carrier. The physical carrier (commonly painting or sculpture) is the medium of expression of the surreal. Thus, an idea is communicable only when the surreal is converted into material terms. The artist's technical problem is how to transform the material with which he works back into the sphere of the spirit.

This two-way transformation proceeds from metaphysical perceptions, for metaphysics is the *search* for the essential nature of reality. And so artistic creation is the metamorphosis of the external physical aspects of a thing into a self-sustaining spiritual reality. Such is the magic act which takes place continuously in the development of a work of art. On this and only on this is creation based.

Still it is not clear what the intrinsic qualities in a medium actually are to make the metamorphosis from the physical into the spiritual possible. Metaphysically, a thing in itself never expresses anything. It is the relation between things that gives meaning to them and that formulates a thought. A thought functions only as a fragmentary part in the formulation of an idea.

A thought that has found a plastic expression must continue to expand in keeping with its own plastic idiom. A plastic idea must be expressed with plastic means just as a musical idea is expressed with musical means, or a literary idea with verbal means. Neither music nor literature are wholly translatable into other art forms; and so a plastic art cannot be created through a superimposed literary meaning. The artist who attempts to do so produces nothing more than a show-booth. He contents himself with visual storytelling. He subjects himself to a mechanistic kind of thinking which disintegrates into fragments.

The plastic expression of one relation must in turn be related to a like expression of another relation if a coherent plastic art is to be the outcome. In this way the expression of a work of art becomes synonymous with the sum of relations and associations organized in terms of the medium of expression by an intuitive artist.

The relative meaning of two physical facts in an emotionally controlled relation always creates the phenomenon of a third fact of a higher order, just as two musical sounds, heard simultaneously create the phenomenon of a third, fourth, or fifth. The nature of this higher third is non-physical. In a sense it is magic. Each such phenomenon always overshadows the material qualities and the limited meaning of the basic factors from which it has sprung. For this reason Art expresses the highest quality of the spirit when it is surreal in nature; or, in terms of the visual arts, when it is of a surreal plastic nature.

Let us explain our philosophical perceptions with the help of a practical example: take a sheet of paper and make a line on it. Who can say whether this line is long or short? Who can say what its direction is? But when, on this same sheet of paper, you make another shorter line, you can see immediately that the first line is the longer one. By placing the second line so that it is not exactly under the first line, you create a sense of movement which will leave no doubt as to the direction in which the first line moves, and in which direction the second is opposed to it.

Was it necessary to enlarge the first line to make it the longer one? We did not have to touch that line or make any change. We gave it meaning through its relation to the new line; and in so doing, we gave simultaneous meaning also to this new line, meaning which it could not have had otherwise. The dominating thought of any relation is always reflected in both directions. But it is the multi-reflex of a particular thought with respect to an over-all idea that finally lifts an artistic expression into the realm of magic. In other words, it is the surreal content of the work that absorbs and overshadows the structure and the physical foundation. The spiritual quality dominates the material.

But, is this all that happened when you made these two lines? You may think so, but that is by no means the case. You started out on an empty piece of paper. The paper is no longer empty. What has happened? Is there nothing but a combination of two lines on an empty sheet of paper? Certainly not! The fact that you placed one line somewhere on the paper created a very definite relationship between this line and the edges of your paper. (You were not aware perhaps that these edges were the first lines of your composition.) By adding another line you not only have a certain tension between the two lines, but also a tension between the unity of these two lines and the outline of your paper. The fact that your two lines, when considered either separately, or as a unit, have a definite relation to the outline, makes the lines and the paper a unified entity which (since lines and paper are physically different) exists entirely in the intellect.

From the beginning, your paper is limited, as all geometrical figures are limited. Within its confines is the complete creative message. Everything you do is definitely related to the paper. The outline becomes an essential part of your composition. Its own meaning, as a limitation, is related to the multi-meanings of your two lines. The more the work progresses, the more it becomes defined or qualified. It increasingly limits itself. Expansion, paradoxically, becomes contraction.

Expansion and contraction in a simultaneous existence is a characteristic of space. Your paper has actually been transformed into space. A sensation of movement and countermovement is simultaneously created through the position of these two lines in their relation to the outline of the paper. Movement and countermovement result in tension. Tensions are the expression of forces. Forces are the expression of actions. In their surreal relationship, the lines may now give the idea of being two shooting stars which move with speed through the universe. Your empty paper has been transformed by the simplest graphic means to a universe in action. This is real magic. So your paper is a world in itself—or you may call it, more modestly, only an object, or simply a picture with a life of its own—a spiritual life—through which it can become a work of art.

Your two lines carry multi-meanings:

They move in relation to each other.

They have tension in themselves.

They express active mutual forces.

This makes them into a living unit.

The position of this unit bears a definite relation to the entire paper.

This in turn creates tensions of a still higher order.

Visual and spiritual movements are simultaneously expressed in these tensions.

They change the meaning of your paper as it defines and embodies space.

Space must be vital and active— a force impelled pictorial space, presented as a spiritual and unified entity, with a life of its own.

This entity must have a life of the spirit without which no art is possible—the life of a creative mind in its sensitive relation to the outer world.

The work of art is firmly established as an independent object; this makes it a picture.

Outside of it is the outer world.

Inside of it, the world of an artist.

A consciousness of limitation is paramount for an expression of the Infinite. Beethoven creates Eternity in the physical limitation of his symphonies. Any limitation can be subdivided infinitely. This involves the problem of time and relativity. A glimpse heavenward at a constellation or even at a single star only *suggests* infinity; actually our vision is limited. We cannot perceive unlimited space; it is immeasurable. The universe, as we know it through our visual experience, is limited. It first came into existence with the formation of matter, and will end with the complete dissolution of matter. Where there is matter and action, there is space.

Pictorial space exists two dimensionally. When the two dimensionality of a picture is destroyed, it falls into parts—it creates the effect of naturalistic space. When a picture conveys only naturalistic space, it represents a special case, a portion of what is felt about three-dimensional experience. This expression of the artist's experience is thus incomplete.

The layman has extreme difficulty in understanding that plastic creation on a flat surface is possible without destroying this flat surface. But it is just this conceptual completeness of a plastic experience that warrants the preservation of the two dimensionality. A plastic approach which is incomplete conceptually will destroy the two dimensionality, and being incomplete in concept, the creation will be inadequate.

Depth, in a pictorial, plastic sense, is not created by the arrangement of objects one after another toward a vanishing point, in the sense of the Renaissance perspective, but on the contrary (and in absolute denial of this doctrine) by the creation of forces in the sense of *push and pull*. Nor is depth created by tonal gradation—(another doctrine of the academician which, at its culmination, degraded the use of color to a mere function of expressing dark and light).

Since one cannot create "real depth" by carving a hole in the picture, and since one should not attempt to create the illusion of depth by tonal gradation, depth as a plastic reality must be two dimensional in a formal sense as well as in the sense of color. "Depth" is not created on a flat surface as an illusion, but as a plastic reality. The nature of the picture plane makes it possible to achieve depth without destroying the two-dimensional essence of the picture plane. Before proceeding, however, the artist must realize the necessity of differentiating between a line and a plane concept.

A plane is a fragment in the architecture of space. When a number of planes are opposed one to another, a spatial effect results. A plane functions in the same manner as the walls of a building. A number of such walls in a given relation creates architectural space in accordance with the idea of the architect who is the creator of this space. Planes organized within a picture create the pictorial space of its composition. In an old master composition, the outline of a figure was considered as a plane and as such the figure became plastically active in the composition. The old masters were plane conscious. This makes their pictures restful as well as vital, irrespective of the dramatic emphasis.

A line concept cannot control pictorial space absolutely. A line may flow freely in and out of space, but cannot independently create the phenomenon of *push and pull* necessary to plastic creation. *Push and pull* are expanding and contracting forces which are activated by carriers in visual motion. Planes are the most important carriers, lines and points less so.

The forces of *push and pull* function three dimensionally without destroying other forces functioning two dimensionally. The movement of a carrier on a flat surface is possible only through an act of shifting left and right or up and down. To create the phenomenon of *push and pull* on a flat surface, one has to understand that by nature the picture plane reacts automatically in the opposite direction to the stimulus received; thus action continues as long as it receives stimulus in the creative process. *Push* answers with *pull* and *pull* with *push*. For example, the inside pressure of a balloon is in balance in every direction. By pressing one side of the balloon, you will disturb this balance, and, as a consequence, the other end will swallow up the amount of pressure applied. Needless to say, this procedure can be reversed. Exactly the same thing can happen to the picture plane in a spiritual sense. When a force is created somewhere in the picture that is intended to be a stimulus in the sense of a *push* the picture plane answers automatically with a force in the sense of *pull* and vice versa.

The function of *push and pull* in respect to form contains the secret of Michelangelo's monumentality or of Rembrandt's universality. At the end of his life and at the height of his capacity, Cezanne understood color as a force of *push and pull*. In his pictures he created an enormous sense of volume, breathing, pulsating, expanding, contracting through his use of color. His watercolors were forever exercises in this direction. Only very great painting becomes so plastically sensitive, for the expression of the deepest in man calls for unexpected and surprising associations.

The graphic arts deal only with basic problems of form. Painting, however, involves a formal problem which depends in its last analysis on the function of color as well as on the essential nature of the picture plane. A painting (which means no more than "forming with color") may embody the same images as does a work of graphic art through the control of form, but it must be realized by very different ways and means since color has an intricate life of its own. To understand this seemingly dual problem of form and color involved in painting, we must first make clear what the intrinsic life of color really is, and what makes this life a vital factor in plastic creation.

Color is a plastic means of creating intervals. Intervals are color harmonics produced by special relationships, or tensions. We differentiate now between formal tensions and color tensions, just as we differentiate in music between counterpoint and harmony. And just as counterpoint and harmony follow their own laws, and differ in rhythm and movement, both the formal tensions and the color tensions have a development of their own in accordance with the inherent laws from which they are separately derived. Both, however, as we have stated, aim toward the realization of the same image. And both deal with the depth problem.

The creative possibilities of color are not limited to plastic expression. Although the composition and function of color are two of the most important factors in determining the qualitative content of a painting, the reciprocal relation of color to color produces a phenomenon of a more mysterious order. This new phenomenon is psychological. A high sensitivity is necessary in order to expand color into the sphere of the surreal without losing creative ground. Color stimulates certain moods in us. It awakens joy or fear in accordance with its configuration. In fact, the whole world, as we experience it visually, comes to us through the mystic realm of color. Our entire being is nourished by it. This mystic quality of color should likewise find expression in a work of art.

One must realize that, apart from considerations of color and form, there are two fundamentally different ways of regarding a medium of expression: one is based on taste only—an approach in which the external physical elements of expression are merely pleasingly arranged. This way results in decoration with no spiritual reaction. Arrangement is not art. The second way is based on the artist's power of empathy, to feel the intrinsic qualities of the medium of expression. Through these qualities the medium comes to life and varies plastically as an idea develops.

The whole field of commercial art and much that comes under the heading of applied art is handled in the first way and is chiefly decorative arrangement. The so called fine arts are handled in the second way to give the total of man's inner self—his spiritual world which he can offer only as an artist in the most profound sense.

There have been two separate revolutions in the visual arts which coincided. A revolution started in the field of the fine arts at the decline of Impressionism, with the birth of Cubism. The Impressionists, who preceded the Cubists, rediscovered the full plastic significance of the picture plane as a two-dimensional entity. The reason for this re-discovery was a search for the entity of light, expressed through color, which resulted in re-establishing the two dimensionality of the picture plane.

Cubism was a revolution in that the artist broke with tradition by changing from a line to a plane concept. The earlier school modeled with color between the outlines of a linear composition. The new school become plane conscious. As already noted, this change occurred as a revolt against the decadent emphasis on taste alone. Having become aware that the revolution in the fine arts carried the key for a vital and unlimited expression, some leaders in the fields of applied art and of architecture discovered that this was also the key for the vitalization of the applied arts. This was the second revolution. With the awareness of the difference between a line concept and a plane concept, the foundation of applied art was newly laid.

It was especially Gropius in Germany, the founder of the Bauhaus in Weimar, later the Bauhaus in Dessau, who called together highly advanced artists like Klee and Kandinsky, in an attempt to make this school the real leader in the rejuvenation of the applied arts, particularly with respect to modern architecture. At this time, however, there was only a vague comprehension of the essential differences which divide and characterize the two fields in the visual arts.

It was the tragedy of the Bauhaus, that, at the beginning of its existence, it confused the concepts of the fine and applied arts. As we have noted, the first must serve the deepest in man. It concerns man's relation to the world as a spiritual being. The second serves only a utilitarian purpose. The Bauhaus, at this time, was primarily concerned with blending art and craftsmanship. The name, Bauhaus, suggested the medieval ideal of the cathedral architect, with whom all the other arts and crafts of the land were not to be sub- but co-ordinated. The Bauhaus, however, soon became aware that its directives had to be adjusted more to the industrial and mechanical needs of our time. From this very moment on, the Bauhaus was on the right track. It understood the revolution which it had started in the field of applied art. The establishment of the Bauhaus in America coincided with this understanding. The conceptive faculty of America's engineering and utilitarian genius was ready to embrace the new ideas in functional design and their eventual standardization.

The new revolution gave an aesthetic foundation to design once again. The aesthetic discoveries of the Bauhaus were mainly directed toward a vital surface animation by abstract design. This does not require plastic empathy—it is only a surface affair, two dimensional and decorative. It requires, however, deep understanding of textural differentiation and pattern contrast and, furthermore, of rhythm and balance in design—these can be sensed in any medium by a sensitive individual.

The idea of the Bauhaus found further expression in so-called Non-Objective art. Klee and Kandinsky are considered to be the leaders of this group. They must not, however, be considered the initiators of the Bauhaus. They gave impetus to its basic idea because the art of each was considered the highest development in pure two-dimensional, plastic perfection.

We should differentiate between decorative, in a plastic sense, and decorative in a non-plastic sense. The works of these two artists are diametrically opposed to ornamentation and decorative, abstract design. The fact that any great plastic work is also decorative in its two-dimensional completeness does not mean that any design on a flat surface is a plastic creation. The phenomenon of plastic movement determines whether or not a work belongs in the category of the fine arts or in the category of the applied arts. It is the greatest injustice done to Mondrian that people who are plastically blind see only decorative design instead of the plastic perfection which characterizes his work. The whole de Stijl group from which Mondrian's art was derived must be considered a protest against such blindness. This group aimed toward the purest plastic perfection.

We have spoken of a seemingly dual problem involved in painting. Only a few very great painters in history have understood how to approach or proceed in this seemingly two-fold concept. I emphasize "seemingly" because this double—or to say it more correctly—this multi-problem characterizes the very nature of painting. Painting at its greatest is a synthesis arrived at by mastering its multi-problems. Only painters of the stature of Rembrandt and El Greco have been artist and painter in one, not only because they have understood how to compose with color, but, at the same time, how to express with it the profoundness of man. Throughout his life, Cezanne struggled for a synthesis. Renoir mastered it in a high degree by instinct. Van Gogh and many others have despaired of it. America possesses great potentialities in the search for creative clarification, though she may look back on a generation entirely misunderstood—the tragic generation of the pioneers of Modern Art.

We have explained that quality, a pure, human value, results from the faculty of empathy, the gift of discerning the mystery of each thing through its own intrinsic life. In this life, an intuitive artist discovers the emotive and vital substance which makes a work of art. In the passage of time, the outward message of a work may lose its initial meaning; the communicative power of its emotive and vital substance, however, will stay alive as long as the work is in existence. The life-giving zeal in a work of art is deeply imbedded in its qualitative substance. The spirit in a work is synonymous with its quality. The *Real* in art never dies, because its nature is predominantly spiritual.

Sculpture

I

We recognize three fundamental categories of sculptural expression:

    sculpture in an applied function—as *decor* and adornment;

    sculpture in an integrated function—as a vital part of architecture;

    sculpture in a sovereign function—as an independent entity with an independent life of its own.

In using the term "sculptural expression," we mean an idea realized with the help of the sculptural medium. A formal sculptural statement embodies a spiritual message in which the whole idea materializes as a new reality in direct ratio to the development of the work.

Sculpture of the first category is merely an object. Its ultimate aesthetic function is decoration. It is applied art.

Sculpture of the second category serves as a fragment in an integrated function. As such it must adapt itself to the idea which it serves. It must provide an aesthetic function in accordance with the idea. Its communicative value is not limited to its physical boundaries. It is a vital integrated part of a vital entity. Relative to architecture, such a work may function as a complete work of art in itself, and at the same time, as an architectural fragment. A column, for example, modified by sculpture, must remain in the formal limits of a cylinder; a bas-relief within the spatial limits of a slab, which is an architectural plane; a sculptured figure, within the spatial limits of the architectural block out of which it is created.

When a sculptured figure has lost its meaning as an architectural block then it belongs in the third category. Such a work must function independently. It represents an entity in itself. Its spiritual sphere does not end with its physical periphery. It has the power to enliven its environment. Its message is all embracing since it is of a metaphysical nature. The body is only the shell—but the shell embodies a spiritual reality.

Every art has its own language. But all media of expression function in the same way—the physical carrier is overshadowed by a relation. The relation creates an overtone. The physical carrier is absorbed by this overtone. The overtone spontaneously transforms the means of creation into a spiritual reality. The mystery of creation is then revealed.

II

Sculpture deals with basic forms. The basic forms are: cubes, cones, spheres and pyramids. Every subject has a characteristic basic form. These forms can be intensified by opposing them to other basic forms. The choice of basic forms is dependent on the artist's feeling for his subject. His feeling develops from comparisons. Comparisons provide a perception of oppositions and relationships. A head is not round or square in itself, it is only so in relation to another basic form which is less round or square. Only through relationship and opposition can "form" be defined in its relative and characteristic proportion.

Measure results from the relation of masses. A sculptural work should not consist of a monotonous series of equal volumes. A differentiation of basic forms and their relative measure is a prerequisite of vital plastic creation.

All basic forms exist as volumes. A volume is a more or less complicated plane formation. The characteristic of a plane is its two-dimensional surface. Planes move around and thereby define a basic form. The manifold movements of all planes surrounding the kernel of a basic form create an active and vital plastic volume.

A plane formation should not destroy the character of the fundamental form, nor should it destroy the general movement.

Every plane has a characteristic depth relation to the kernel of a fundamental form, as well as to each of the other planes. The basic forms either expand or contract depending on the various depth relations. In this way surface tensions are created—they express the inner life of an existing or created form. A multitude of extended or contracted forms, conceived on the basis of the fundamental form, gives the work its character.

We have defined a physical volume as a more or less complicated plane formation. A multitude of such volumes offers, of course, considerably more difficulties for plastic analysis. The question arises: How do planes, belonging to different volumes or to a multitude of volumes, function in relation to each other? A plane not only functions in relation to its own volume, but also functions continuously with the entire plastic unit. This means that the relationships of a given plane are not limited to the volume to which it belongs, but that such relationships exist also with planes of different volumes as well.

Volumes penetrate each other and in this way are no longer single formations. When two or more volumes penetrate one another, a totally new form is created. In this new form, the constructive elements—in our case, the elementary volumes—seem either partly or totally absorbed. They give way to a totally new appearance. An entire new being comes into existence and, simultaneously with it, a new space constellation.

The life of the new being is the life of the new space constellation. The forces of the one are conditioned by the forces of the other. The one creates the tensions in which forms exist, the other creates the tensions in which space exists. Both are mutually dependent upon each other. Only the sum of both creates a plastic and vital sculptural entity.

Through penetration, space is created in its entirety—every portion of space results from it. The forces of penetration are perpetually at work in shaping the world constantly anew. In the eternal cycle of perpetual change, life manifests its continuity.

The phenomenon of penetration embraces the whole universe. Whether or not he is conscious of it the artist deals with it in feeling. No vital function, no rhythm in which life manifests itself is conceivable without it. No physical forces, no mental elaboration, nor interpretation, no association, nor metaphysical speculation, is thinkable, had nature not provided a key for absorption and continuation in the act of penetration.

III

Movement in sculpture does not actually exist in point of time, but the experience of movement is sensed in the limitation of the medium. The limitations of sculpture are found in a coherence of opposing forces related to positive and negative space.

Basic forms are positive space volumes; negative space is created through the opposition of these positive space volumes. Positive space is life fulfilled—negative space is force impelled. Both exist simultaneously —both condition each other—neither is conceivable without the other. Only the simultaneous existence of positive and negative space creates a plastic unity.

All volumes can be considered as having imaginary vertical and horizontal axes. All volumes move around such axes. And each of these axes can be brought in opposition to the other. The result is movement and counter-movement in spatial opposition.

    (a) Movement and counter-movement create negative space as a volume. Volume is space.
    (b) Movement and counter-movement create tensions.

(c) Space is enlivened by tension.

(d) Tensions are the expression of forces.

(e) Forces are the expression of life.

The continuity of movement is neither limited to the object nor to its counterpart, negative space, but is dependent upon both of them. All planes must be related to create the life-giving tension in an object and the force-impelled spatial tensions outside and surrounding the object. The surface tension breathes the inner life of a form; the spatial tension is the life of the plastic unit.

Since the continuity of movement depends upon both positive and negative space, and since tensions result from movement and counter-movement, no one tension can exist without its counterpart.

It is the intensity of movement and counter-movement which differentiates one tension from another and which, in the end, creates the rhythmic play in which a plastic work exists.

Opposing forces function within the limits of the static and the dynamic. The dynamic is resolved into ultimate static. Thus a plastic work exists, powerful, limited in space, as the result of a multitude of opposing functions, and in this way summarizes time as a simultaneous experience.

IV

A complete plastic unity necessarily creates a unity of light. In a sculptural work, actual form should always function in relation to light.

Every plane has the faculty of reflecting and absorbing light. Since every plane has a different spatial position with respect to the light source, each plane differentiates light according to its function of creating plastic unity. In this way, depth is created and emphasized.

We see two-dimensionally. We have learned with the help of our other senses to interpret two-dimensionality as a three-dimensional experience; reality comes to us as a visual experience with the help of appearance, and appearance speaks to us through the element of light. Light creates forms and shapes which do not actually exist. They exist only as appearances. A curved plane, although it seems to be a single shape, cannot function as a single plane, because it refracts light like a multitude of planes.

Depth absorbs light, a protruding form reflects light. A sculptured work should be balanced in the reflected intensity and the absorption of light. Such balance is achieved at the point where the greatest expansion of the surface tensions are counter-balanced by the contracting forces of the negative space.

A sculptured work which is not balanced in this way does not offer absolute two-dimensionality from every angle of observation—as it should—but rather it expresses an irritating unbalanced three-dimensional effect, since it is incomplete in its three-dimensional realization.

Another variation of light is created through the surface treatment of the plane. Such a treatment is possible within the potentiality of the material used. Every material has a particular substantial structure, which causes it to be soft or hard, shiny or dull, rough or smooth, etc. Every material has also a texture and a color of its own. These inherent qualities of the material must be surely sensed and understood in regard to the surface motivation in the creation of light.

Concavity in sculpture demands convexity, reflection calls for its counterpart, absorption, intensity requires depth. A sculptural work can be shown under almost every circumstantial illumination, because the inherent relations in its construction are unchangeable, once the work is completed. Different illuminations only change the appearance, but do not affect the inner relations. These relations always respond in the sense in which they were conceived, in spite of changing outside circumstances. Thus a sculptural work speaks to us as a plastic entity, as the sum of its relations, through our perception of its unity of light.

Within the spatial limitation of the work, form and light function together to achieve a co-existent light unity and plastic unity. The rhythmic integration of all the functions of sculpture expresses the subjective experience of the artist as a creator.

Painting and Culture

It is generally accepted that one cannot make an artist, but that one can teach art; that every art is ruled by a conception of order—a harmony and counterpoint, which has in practice arisen out of the nature of the art itself.

The harmony and counterpoint of creative drawing and painting has been lost, since the Renaissance, in the straining after superficialities and copying of appearances.

The formal elements of painting are line, plane, volume and the resulting formal complexes. These are elements of construction which, when properly utilized, produce form.

The aim of art is to vitalize form. This vitality arises as the result of organic relationships between the formal elements, which in turn arise through the separation and relation of qualities inherent in the medium—in short, color and light integrated into planes.

Nature exists on the one hand as three dimensional form, with variations, relations and separations as to the quantities and qualities within its essential unity. On the other hand, the picture plane exists two dimensionally, yet capable of separation into visual planes.

The knowledge of reality, achieved by means of the complete sensory equipment, must be expressed artistically in terms of a medium which appeals to the memory of all sensory experience—but only through the eye.

While the experience of nature is achieved by various sensory approaches, the experience of a picture is achieved by means of a visual impression alone. The picture stands or falls on its appeal to the eye alone, but this stimulus calls up necessary associations with qualities which have been perceived through other senses and stored in the subconscious, if the observer is sensitively endowed.

In order that visual stimulation may be assisted by memory, the picture must, with this purpose in view, present elements more definitely adapted and ordered than the visual appearance of nature alone.

Light and shade do not always convey the truth about form realized in actual experiences of nature. Only by the aid of our other senses do we gain a proper understanding of the particular form we have before us.

When we lift shapes out of their numerous relationships in the natural world or from the mental associations formed by our senses, we must endow them with an authenticity which is pictorial rather than natural. The picture must be consistent within itself in order to avoid false illusions arising from new relations within the frame of the picture. So the process of re-creating reality is not based upon a simple reproduction of nature.

It is evident that art may be taught only upon the basis of a highly developed sensitivity for quality.

The difference between the layman who understands art and the man who creates art is that the layman, or the critic, out of receptive experience, shares passively what the artist, out of productive experience, feels and creates.

Creation is dominated by three absolutely different factors: first, nature, which affects us by its laws; second, the artist who creates a spiritual contact with nature and with his materials; and third, the medium of expression through which the artist translates his inner world.

The creative process lies not in imitating, but in paralleling nature—translating the impulse received from nature into the medium of expression, thus vitalizing this medium. The picture should be alive, the statue should be alive and every work of art should be alive.

Every work of art is the product of the artist's power for conscious feeling, and of his sensitivity to life-in-nature and life within the limits of his medium.

The depth of an artistic creation is a question of human development. The deeper the human content, the deeper the understanding of the medium.

The *Ninth Symphony* of Beethoven and any polonaise start from the same musical principle. The contrasts lie in the difference of the human content. One is a world, the other is only an element in a world.

A profound interpretation of a symphony does not demand technical facility as much as it demands a deep human feeling for its content. The highest technique is evolved from this feeling.

The possibility of the medium is as unlimited as are the possibilities of the human capacity for comprehension.

It is the aim of every cultural pursuit to enrich and to give deeper content to life.

Genius is gifted with a vitality which is expended in the enrichment of life through the discovery of new worlds of feeling. Art and science create a balance to material life and enlarge the world of living experience. Art leads to a more profound concept of life, because art itself is a profound expression of feeling.

The artist is born, and art is the expression of his overflowing soul. Because his soul is rich, he cares comparatively little about the superficial necessities of the material world; he sublimates the pressure of material affairs in an artistic experience.

Art is something absolute, something positive, which gives power just as food gives power.

While creative science is mental food, art is the satisfaction of the soul.

A material world which excludes art will remain a troubled world. The materialist flees from the crying need of his unsatisfied spirit to the drive of the "daily grind." Since his physical satisfaction does not necessarily include spiritual satisfaction, the sum total of his living remains unsatisfied. Such a man suffers an inner emptiness, and soon cannot endure thoughtfulness, nor the products of contemplation.

Spinoza says, "Only contemplated experience becomes real experience," which is the reverse of "Let's go places and do things." The materialist flees through an insecure world of shifting illusions, finding no permanent reality.

It takes intelligence and training, self-discipline and fine sensibility, to gain renewed life through leisure occupation. America now suffers spiritual poverty, and art must come more fully into American life before her leisure can become culture.

Art teaching has a meaning for America, and should be more general and more significant. The problem of civilizing this enormous country is not finished. The teaching of art must be directed toward the enrichment of the student's life. The teacher must be a guiding personality for the student, and develop his sensibility and his power for "feeling into" animate, or inanimate things, with sympathy.

It is essential that the teacher himself have the power of quick sympathy and understanding of the unsure student. Such power should be developed like every other human attribute. The problem of art teaching is not limited to the problem of artistic development itself, but includes the problems of how to produce artists, comprehending teachers, art understanding in general, and art enjoyment in particular.

The general misunderstanding of a work of art is often due to the fact that the key to its spiritual content and technical means is missed. Unless the observer is trained to a certain degree in the artistic idiom, he is apt to search for things which have little to do with the aesthetic content of a picture. He is likely to look for purely representational values when the emphasis is really upon music-like relationships.

Everything rhythmically organic is true. Everything which results from the proper feeling for rhythmically organized spiritual units is true and alive—alive within itself. When we lose the sense for such true beauty we lose our natural sense for the rich flavor of life, which is the basis for all inspirational work.

Things generally taken for beautiful are nothing other than the product of frozen, stereotyped taste, bound by sterile rules and by purely exterior judgment.

The two dimensionality in oriental visual art, so often copied without the understanding of its plastic content, is an example of such mechanical stylization. Copying of any style, without understanding the vital qualities of its creative impulses, must result in sterile work.

Literary content is objective "story value."

Plastic value in art arises as a result of relations of volumes in space.

The literary artist is apt to stop with the "story value" of the object.

The plastic artist is concerned with the music-like relationships of plastic units just as the musical artist is concerned with the harmonic relationships of musical units.

The plastic artist may or may not be concerned with presenting a superficial appearance of reality, but he is always concerned with the presentation—if not the representation—of the plastic values of reality.

The difference between the arts arises because of the difference in the nature of the mediums of expression and in the emphasis induced by the nature of each medium. Each means of expression has its own order of being, its own units.

The key to understanding lies in the appreciation of the limitations, qualities, and possibilities of variation and relation of these presentational elements.

Unless one recognizes letters, one cannot read.

Speech has arisen through the need for expression. Certain factors have contributed to making it the paramount utilitarian method of expression. There are ideas and things expressible in words, but there are experiences better expressed in music. The person with no musical ear, or without discipline in the language of music, lacks the key to the door of the world of music experience. But we live in a world of volume and space; it is hard to conceive of the person who is space-blind or volume deaf. The great majority of people have the means of approach to plastic beauty as part of their natural equipment. The teacher can develop this natural endowment as Necessity, the greatest teacher, has developed speech.

Teachers are those who, by enforced discipline, shorten the road to understanding, but they can work only by developing natural endowment.

There is a world of visual beauty open to the one willing to undergo the practice and striving necessary to an understanding of its language.

This world is as important culturally as is the world of words or of music. My ideal is to form and to paint as Schubert sings his songs and as Beethoven creates his world in sounds. That is to say, creation of one's own inner world through the same human and artistic discipline.

An inner sensation can find external expression only through a spiritual realization.

When the impulses which stir us to profound emotion are integrated with the medium of expression, every interview of the soul may become art. This is contingent upon the mastery of the medium. A pictorial decorative arrangement is dictated only by taste—which is, after all, only a passing fad, or fashion. Pictorial homogeneity of the composition (plastic unity) is developed by lawfully governed inner necessities. These inner necessities are dictated by the nature of the medium, and from the orchestration of its inner qualities arise formal movement, tensions, intervals, complementary relations, contrasts, and complexes.

The impulse of nature, fused through the personality of the artist by laws arising from the particular nature of the medium, produces the rhythm and the personal expression of a work. Then the life of the composition becomes a spiritual unity.

Artistic expression and appreciation is necessary to a complete, balanced life, and must be an integral part of any enduring national or racial culture.

When America adds a developed culture to its economic richness it will be one of the happiest countries in the world. Providing leadership by teachers and support of developing artists is a national duty, an insurance of spiritual solidarity. What we do for art, we do for ourselves and for our children and the future.

Excerpts from the Teaching of Hans Hofmann

On the Aim and Nature of Art

The aim of art, so far as one can speak of an aim at all, has always been the same; the blending of experience gained in life with the natural qualities of the art medium.

Artistic intuition is the basis for confidence of the spirit. Art is a reflection of the spirit, a result of introspection, which finds expression in the nature of the art medium.

When the artist is well equipped with conscious feeling, memory and balanced sensibilities, he intensifies his concepts by penetrating his subject and by condensing his experience into a reality of the spirit complete in itself. Thus he creates a new reality in terms of the medium.

The medium becomes the work of art, but only when the artist is intuitive and at the same time masters its essential nature and the principles which govern it.

A work of art is a world in itself reflecting senses and emotions of the artist's world.

Just as a flower, by virtue of its existence as a complete organism, is both ornamental and self-sufficient as to color, form, and texture, so art, because of its singular existence, is more than mere ornament.

On The Limitations of Physical Elements

Every real object possesses form, color and texture; and the manner in which these basic qualities are related characterizes that specific object.

This relationship is the external expression of an orderly internal process of development. And so it is with art which is the final result of an internal process of development.

The metamorphosis which takes place when an experience is translated into a medium of expression is a plastic act controlled by inherent but limited qualities of that medium. The infinite can be created only on the basis of such a limitation.

The universe itself is limited in its complexity. Only the absolute nothing is unlimited, unthinkable, unseizable, shapeless, forceless, non-existent.

The structure of a picture depends on the limitations of the picture plane.

The first line of the composition establishes the creative format. The physical limitations of a picture become the start and the finish of the spirit's communication.

On Standards and Values

We are connected with our own age if we recognize ourselves in relation to outside events; and we have grasped its spirit when we influence the future.

A person seeking purely external values never posesses true inner greatness unless the external expression is but a final stage of deep inner development, of introspection. The only values which make a work of art great are emotional and sensory. Sensory raw material blended to a spiritual unity through legitimate use of the medium is art. The sensitive artist may indefinitely develop the spatial meaning of any sized format.

The width of a line may present the idea of infinity. An epigram may contain a world. In the same way, a small picture format may be much more living, much more leavening, stirring, awakening than square yards of wall space.

Images which differ only by a fraction of a millimeter on the two dimensional surface of a picture may, in certain circumstances, become the expression of artistic infinity.

The spiritual and mental content of a painting is found only in its pictorial quality and not in the allegory, or in the symbolic meaning, presented by objects.

Inner greatness, pictorially, is determined and limited by the relative degree to which the pictorial effect of depth, in contrast to the illusion of depth, serves the artist's purpose.

The word decorative, used in a naturalistic sense, applies only to the representation of objects arranged by a fanciful and arbitrary taste and subordinated to an illustrative meaning. Burdening the canvas with propaganda, or history, does not make the painting a better work of art. Such burdening, in the majority of cases, decreases the quality of the work. It destroys its living, vivid relations and with it the swinging, vibrating space proper to visual art. To evaluate a painting, all literary or journalistic considerations should be abandoned entirely.

We must discriminate between decorative in a pictorial sense and decorative in a naturalistic sense. A pictorially decorative effect is achieved by rhythmic relations contrasted and conditioned by space. This leads to abstraction, wherein objective values are by no means necessarily eliminated, but, on the contrary, are made more effective by rhythmic relation. Color and form then function as symbols.

An artist is valued for his personal interpretive insight and not for his conformity to traditional patterns. So it is always an indication of uncertain knowledge if, when judging a work of art, one compares the work of one artist with that of another. Quality is quality wherever found. The artist must follow his inner urge, independent of fads and fashions.

On Creation

The encompassing, creative mind recognizes no boundaries. The mind has ever brought new spheres under its control.

All our experiences culminate in the perception of the universe as a whole with man as its center.

Visual experience cannot be based on feeling or perception alone. Feelings and perceptions which are not sublimated by the essence of things lose themselves in the sentimental.

Every deep artistic expression is the product of a conscious feeling for reality. This concerns both the reality of nature and the reality of the intrinsic life of the medium of expression.

The difference between art produced by children and great works of art is that one is approached through the purely subconscions and emotional, and the other retains a consciousness of experience as the work develops and is emotionally enlarged through the greater command of the expression-medium.

To experience visually, and to transform our visual experience into plastic terms, requires the faculty of empathy.

Dreams and reality are united in our imagination. The artist possesses the means to create only after he has effective command of his faculty of empathy which he must develop simultaneously with his imaginative capacity.

The process of creation is based upon two metaphysical factors: (1) upon the power to experience through the faculty of empathy, and (2) upon the spiritual interpretation of the expression-medium as a result of such powers. Concept and execution condition each other equally. The greater the concept, the more profound and intensive will the spiritual animation of the expression-medium generally be and, consequently, the greater will be the impressiveness and importance of the work.

We distinguish two technical factors in creative painting: (1) the symphonic animation of the picture plane, (as in the so-called art of easel painting or print making, etching, engraving, and other forms of drawing which may suggest color); and (2) the decorative animation of the picture plane, as in so-called mural painting. Truly considered, however, the names "easel picture" and "mural picture" express purely external differences. Philosophically, every work which possesses intrinsic greatness is at once decorative and symphonically focused and integrated.

Every creative act requires elimination and simplification. Simplification results from a realization of what is essential.

The mystery of plastic creation is based upon the dualism of the two dimensional and the three dimensional.

On Experience and Appearances

Appearance is two dimensional. Reality is three dimensional. Hence the conceptions of three dimensionality and two dimensionality are identified with the terms reality and appearance. The process of seeing is based upon appearance—whereas experience is based upon the effect of the appearance on us. The resultant effect is something entirely different from the appearance.

Spatial nature is not two dimensional—it only appears to be so—and the appearance is not three dimensional, but rather it has the effect on us of being so. Emotionally, we experience space as being three dimensional.

If things are other than they appear, then the limited capacity of our senses must be united through an inner vision. Empathy results from this inner vision.

By using the faculty of empathy, our emotional experiences can be gathered together as an inner perception by which we can comprehend the essence of things beyond mere, bare sensory experience. The physical eye sees only the shell and the semblance; the inner eye, however, sees to the core and grasps the opposing forces and the coherence of things. In their relations and their connections, these things present us with effects which are not three dimensionally real but are supersensory and thereby transcendental. As far as we are concerned, then, the essence of things lies in super-sensory conceptions.

We control reality through our senses, and all our ideas of the world go back originally to our emotional experiences.

Nature limited our senses wisely, because only on the basis of this limitation are our sensory impressions spiritually attainable to us as experiences.

On Relation

Monumentality is an affair of relativity. The truly monumental can only come about by means of the most exact and refined relation between parts. Since each thing carries both a meaning of its own and an associated meaning in relation to something else—its essential value is relative. We speak of the mood we experience when looking at a landscape. This mood results from the relation of certain things rather than from their separate actualities. This is because objects do not in themselves possess the total effect they give when interrelated.

Similarly the representation element (subject matter) and the presentation elements (line, plane, color) do not separately produce the same effects as when related in a finally created work. The effect produced is the quintessence of the relation.

The mind uses subject matter as a vehicle for the creation of a surreal effect. The sum total of such surreal effects forms the emotional substance of a work.

It is a mistake to believe that the representation of objects excludes aesthetic profoundness. In my opinion, the very opposite is true. The greatness of aesthetic form which the artist creates may culminate in a pictorial realization of objects without any harm to the aesthetic development of the work. The works of the old masters are examples.

The artist who works independently of the chance appearance of nature uses the accumulation of experience gained from nature as the source of his inspiration. He faces the same aesthetic problems in regard to his medium as the artist who works directly from nature. It makes no difference whether his work is naturalistic or abstract; every visual expression follows the same fundamental laws.

Each expression-medium has a life of its own. Regulated by certain laws, it can be mastered only by intuition during the act of creating. It is in the nature of the laws which govern every expression-medium that two separate entities, related through empathy, always produce a higher third of a purely spiritual nature. The spiritual third manifests itself as quality which carries an emotional content. This quality is the opposite of illusion; it is a reality of the spirit. Spiritual qualities influence each other according to the way (creation-direction) in which they become related.

This perception leads necessarily to the concept of an "interval" art. An interval results from relationship. A relation requires at least two material carriers to produce a super-imposed higher "surreal" as the meaning of the relation. A mystic overtone now overshadows the carrier. Its coming into existence is the exact equivalent of the relation. Being of a higher order, only these ultra, dominating relations can give a spiritual character to the work. This spiritual character determines the nature of the final plastic expression.

There is only a very limited relation between scientific laws and the creative process. The first deal with experiences that occur repeatedly in the same manner. Creation occurs through progress from one result to another. A work of art goes through many phases of development, but in each phase it is always a work of art. (Therein lies the importance of sketches.) A work of art is finished, from the point of view of the artist, when feeling and perception have resulted in a spiritual synthesis.

On the Medium of Expression

An idea can only be materialized with the help of a medium of expression, the inherent qualities of which must be surely sensed and understood in order to become the carrier of an idea. The idea is transformed, adapted to, and carried by the inner quality of the medium, not by its external aspect. This explains why the same formative idea can be expressed in a number of different mediums.

An idea to be expressed may be based upon naturalistic experience, fantasy, or abstract concepts. All these sources generate impulses in the mind which may be transformed and given expression through corresponding vibrations within the expression-medium.

The intensity of enlivenment which the expression-medium finally reaches depends solely on the artist's faculty to experience emotionally, which, in its turn, determines the degree of spiritual projection into the nature of the expression-medium. The enlivenment of the expression-medium is the prerequisite of a plastic creation. The question of "What shall be expressed?" is always anticipated by this requirement.

From the very start of his studies an artist who works from nature faces a double problem. He must learn to see (it is amazing what people do not see) and he must learn to interpret his visual experience as a plastic experience. This will not yet enable him to create, for the act of creation is bound to a medium of expression. He must interpret the plastic nature of the medium of expression and translate his experience in accordance with it. This is the meaning of plastic creation.

The artist who disregards plastic creation will be an imitator, not a creator; his work will have no aesthetic foundation.

On Pictorial Laws

Painting possesses fundamental laws. These laws are dictated by fundamental perceptions. One of these perceptions is: the essence of the picture is the picture plane. The essence of the picture plane is its two-dimensionality. The first law is then derived: the picture plane must be preserved in its two-dimensionality throughout the whole process of creation until it reaches its final transformation in the completed picture. And this leads to the second law: the picture must achieve a three-dimensional effect, distinct from illusion, by means of the creative process. These two laws apply both to color and to form.

On The Picture Plane

Three dimensional objects in nature are recorded optically as two dimensional images. These images are identified with the two dimensional quality of the picture plane.

The most complete representation of three dimensionality, in which all the three dimensional fragments are summarized in an entity, results in pictorial two dimensionality.

The act of creation agitates the picture plane, but if the two dimensionality is lost the picture reveals holes and the result is not pictorial, but a naturalistic imitation of nature.

The plane is the creative element of all the plastic arts, painting, sculpture, architecture and related arts. Colors, commonly color bearing planes, are creative elements in painting.

On Line and Plane

A work based only on a line concept is scarcely more than illustration; it fails to achieve pictorial structure. Pictorial structure is based on a plane concept. The line originates in the meeting of two planes. The course of a spatially conceived line develops from different positions in a multitude of planes. Only in a mathematical sense is a line, in itself, thinkable. In a creative sense, the line is to be considered as the carrier of a multiple meaning, since it results from the merging of planes. The line divides, combines, flows. The line and the plane are the vehicles for free orientation.

We can lose ourselves in a multitude of lines, if through them we lose our sense for the planes; we can lose ourselves among planes if we do not perceive their relation to volumes. And we can still be confused by a multitude of volumes if our perception is not strictly limited by the concept of a spatial unity.

On Space

The experience of space depends upon understanding the "living" coherence of things.

It depends upon subjective feeling for the impulses which emanate from a unity of plastic elements.

Form exists through space and space through form. Form should not exist for itself since it represents only part of space. Space, through the existence of objects, becomes tripartite. We differentiate between the space in front of an object, the space within an object, and the space in back of an object. Space within an object is limited. Space in front of and behind an object suggests infinity.

Space discloses itself to us through volumes. "Objects" are positive space. Negative space results from the relation of objects. Negative space is as concrete to the artist as is objective-positive space, and possesses an equal three dimensional effectiveness. Both supplement each other, both resolve into a unity of space.

Two dimensional expression can be creative only by the coexistence of positive and negative space.

We differentiate between the life-fulfilled form and the force-impelled space, which are, in turn, subjected to the static and the dynamic.

We recognize the static as the sum total of the dynamic, just as we recognize the two dimensional as the sum total of the three dimensional.

There can be nothing static which excludes the dynamic and vice versa, and nothing plastically two dimensional which excludes the three dimensional. In this way, we comprehend nature as a unity of opposing and contracting forces.

Form must be balanced by space. Form exists because of space and space exists because of form; thus space and form exist together in a three dimensional unity which is plastically represented by the two dimensional unity of the picture plane.

Space expands and contracts in the tensions and functions through which it exists. Space is not a static, inert thing. Space is alive; space is dynamic; space is imbued with movement expressed by forces and counterforces; space vibrates and resounds with color, light and form in the rhythm of life.

On Movement

Life does not exist without movement and movement does not exist without life. Movement is the expression of life. All movements are of a spatial nature. The continuation of movement throughout space is rhythm. Thereby rhythm is the expression of life in space.

Movement develops from depth sensation. There are movements into space and movements forward, out of space, both in form, and in color.

The product of movement and counter-movement is tension. When tension—working strength—is expressed, it endows the work of art with the living effect of coordinated, though opposing, forces.

Movement, as we experience it, can take a two or a three dimensional course. Movement on a picture plane can only take a two dimensional course. Three dimensional movement can be established upon the picture plane only as two dimensional, for one cannot produce actual depth on the picture plane but only the sensation of depth.

For the same reason, one cannot produce actual motion on the picture plane but only the sensation of motion. Depth and motion find formal expression in the shifting of planes and lines within the plane of the picture.

The tension of movement and counter-movement, achieved through plastic order and unity, parallels the artist's life experience and his artistic and human discipline. It arouses a sympathetic response in the spirit of the observer. The balance of many contrasting factors produces a many-faceted, yet unified, life.

A plastic presentation which is not dominated by movement and rhythm is a dead form and, therefore, inexpressive. Form is the shell of life. Form discloses itself to us as a living thing in its surface tensions. These tensions are kept under the spell of living forces. Only in the fullness of life does a form present its greatest surface tension. The form shrinks and dissolves when life ends, and cold unanimated space ensues. When all form dissolves, unpresentable nothingness remains.

On Light and Color

We recognize visual form only by means of light, and light only by means of form, and we further recognize that color is an effect of light in relation to form and its inherent texture. In nature, light creates color; in painting, color creates light.

In symphonic painting, color is the real building medium. "When color is richest, form is fullest." This declaration of Cezanne's is a guide for painters.

Swinging and pulsating form and its counterpart, resonating space, originate in color intervals. In a color interval, the finest differentiations of color function as powerful contrasts. A color interval is comparable to the tension created by a form relation. What a tension signifies in regard to form, an interval signifies in regard to color; it is a tension between colors that makes color a plastic means.

A painting must have form and light unity. It must light up from the inside through the intrinsic qualities which color relations offer. It must not be illuminated from the outside by superficial effects. When it lights up from the inside, the painted surface breathes, because the interval relations which dominate the whole cause it to oscillate and to vibrate.

A painted surface must retain the transparency of a jewel which stands as a prototype of exactly ordered form, on the one hand, and as a prototype of the highest light emanation on the other.

The Impressionists led painting back to the two dimensional in the picture through the creation of a light unity, whereas their attempt to create atmosphere and spatial effectiveness by means of color, resulted in the impregnation of their works with the quality of translucence which became synonymous with the transparency of the picture plane.

Light must not be conceived as illumination—it forces itself into the picture through color development. Illumination is superficial. Light must be created. In this manner alone is the balance of light possible.

The formation of a light unity becomes identified with the two dimensionality of the picture. Such a formation is based on comprehending light complexities. Color unity, in the same manner, is identified with the two dimensionality of the picture. It results from color tensions created by color intervals. Thus the end product of all color intervals is two dimensionality.

Spatial and formal unity and light and color unity create the plastic two dimensionality of the picture.

Since light is best expressed through differences in color quality, color should not be handled as a tonal gradation, to produce the effect of light.

The psychological expression of color lies in unexpected relations and associations.

On Enjoyment

"Aesthetic enjoyment is caused by the perception of hidden laws.... aesthetic enjoyment is joy in itself, released from subordination to any purpose; therefore, it embraces the enjoyment of nature and the enjoyment of art both." (Walter Rathenau: *Notes on Art Philosophy.*) The aim of art is always to provide such joy for us in every form of expression. The faculty to enjoy rests with the observer.

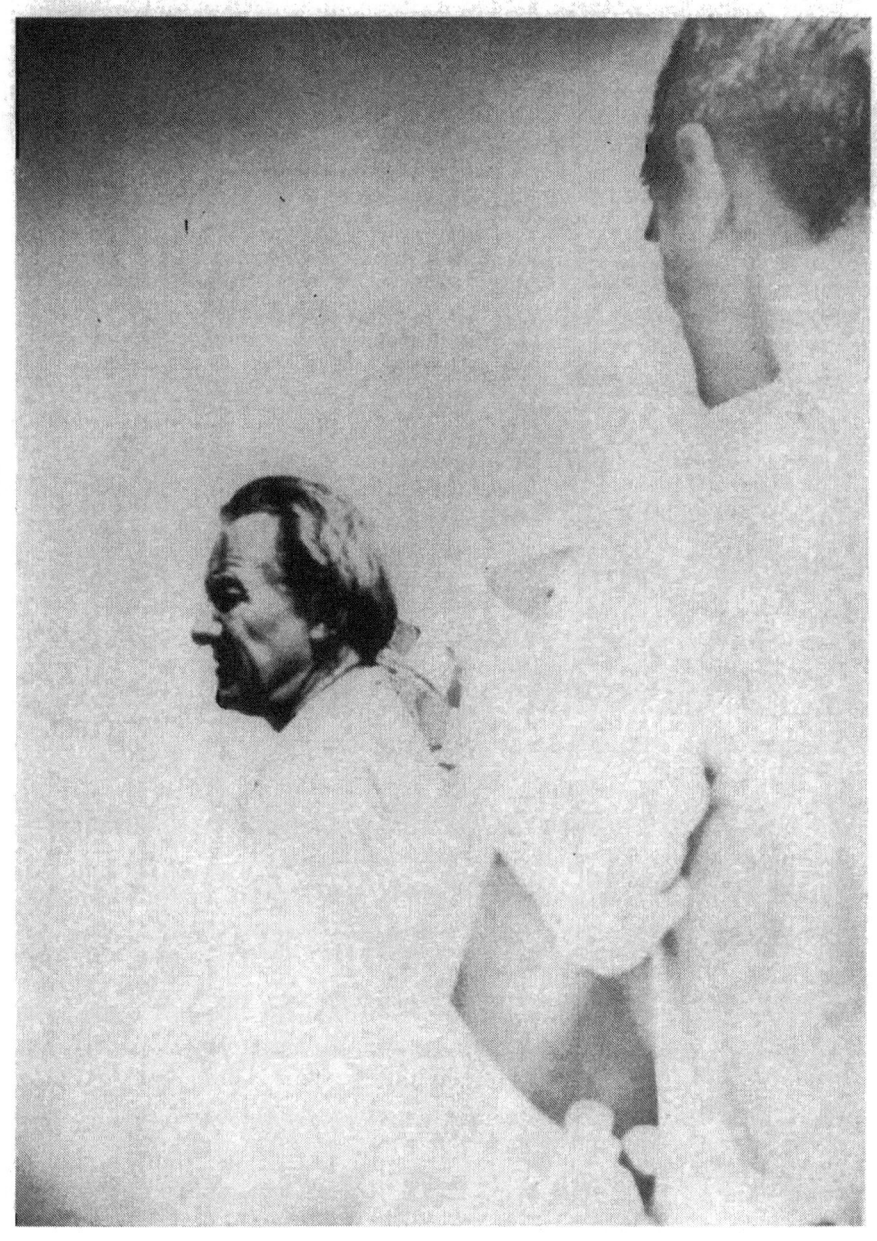

Teacher and Students, Provincetown, 1940

Terms

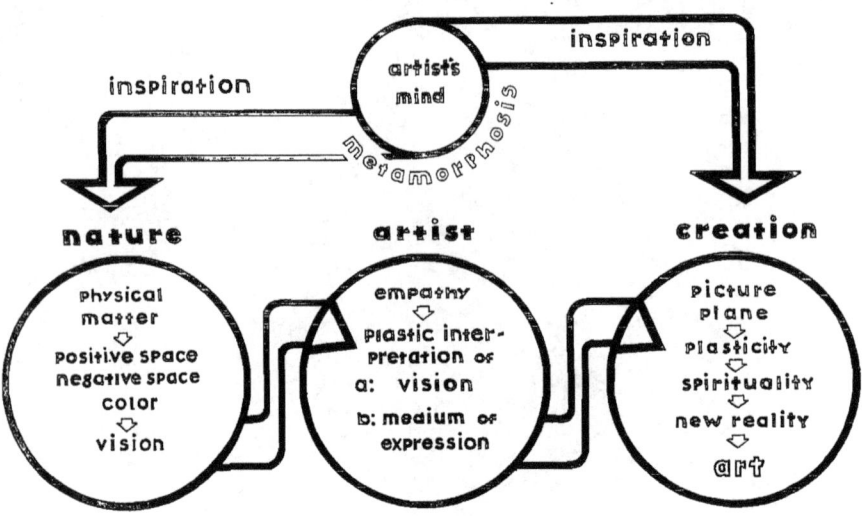

Nature:	the source of all inspiration.
	Whether the *artist* works directly from nature, from memory, or from fantasy, nature is always the source of his creative impulses.
The Artist:	an agent in whose mind nature is transformed into a new *creation*.
	The artist approaches his problems from a metaphysical standpoint. His intuitive faculty of sensing the inherent qualities of things dominates his creative instinct.
Creation:	a synthesis, from the artist's standpoint, of matter, space and color.
	Creation is not a reproduction of observed fact.
Positive Space:	the presence of visible matter.

Negative Space: the configuration, or "constellation," of the voids between and around portions of visible matter.

Color: in a scientific sense, a particular state of light; in an artistic sense, the perception of plastic and psychological differences in the quality of light.

These differences are conceived as color *intervals* which are similar to *tensions*, the expression of related forces between two or more solid forms.

In nature, light creates the sensation of color; in a picture, color creates light.

Vision: the stimulus of the optic nerve by light; artistically, the awareness of variations in the nature of this stimulus which enables one to distinguish positive and negative space and color.

Empathy: the imaginative projection of one's own consciousness into another being, or thing. In visual experience, it is the intuitive faculty to sense qualities of formal and spatial relations, or tensions, and to discover the plastic and psychological qualities of form and color.

Expression Medium: the material means by which ideas and emotions are given visible form.

Each expression medium has a nature and life of its own according to which creative impulses are visualized. The artist must not only interpret his experience of nature creatively, but he must be able to translate his feeling for nature into a creative interpretation of the *expression medium*. To explore the nature of the medium is part of the understanding of nature, as well as part of the process of creation.

Picture Plane: the plane, or surface, on which the picture exists.

The essence of the picture plane is flatness. Flatness is synonymous with two-dimensionality.

Plasticity: the transference of three-dimensional experience to two dimensions. A work of art is plastic when its pictorial message is integrated with the picture plane and when nature is embodied in terms of the qualities of the *expression medium*.

Spirituality: the emotional and intellectual synthesis of relationships perceived in nature, rationally, or intuitively.

Spirituality in an artistic sense should not be confused with religious meaning.

Reality: artistically, an awareness.

There are two kinds of reality: physical reality, apprehended by the senses, and spiritual reality created emotionally and intellectually by the conscious or subconscious powers of the mind.

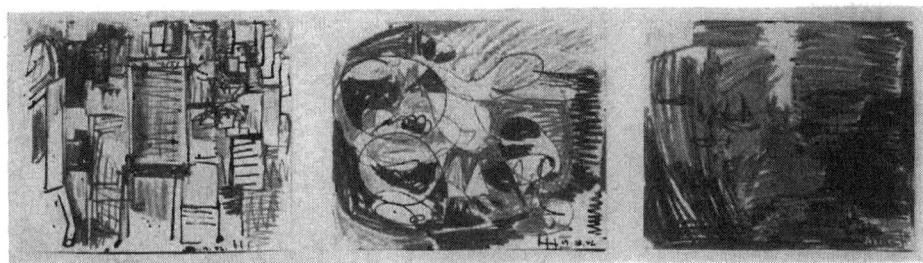

LANDSCAPE STUDIES, Provincetown, 1942

These drawings emphasize in a way not possible by means of conventional illustration quite distinct outlooks toward physical reality which, in varying degree, are recognizable in much of Hofmann's painting. They are expressed in terms of an angular, strict, architectural style; an organic, rhythmic style; and a free, indefinite, amorphous style. Hofmann sees in these differences opposing, yet reconcilable forces — basic moods of nature. He is constantly readjusting and re-evaluating them, and directing his work towards achieving, thereby, a better understanding of nature. The search for the *real*, like the conception of infinity, is unending.

HANS HOFMANN—*at Provincetown, 1940*

MRS. HOFMANN—*with Chang, 1940*

Appendix

A visual catalogue of the retrospective exhibition of Hans Hofmann at the Addison Gallery, 1948

NOTE: In spite of their microscopic size, it is hoped that the following illustrations will have a greater value than the mere listing of relatively meaningless titles, both as a matter of record and as evidence of the creative variety from which the illustrations, pp. 17-45, have been selected.

PART I: THE EVOLUTION OF HOFMANN'S ABSTRACT PAINTING

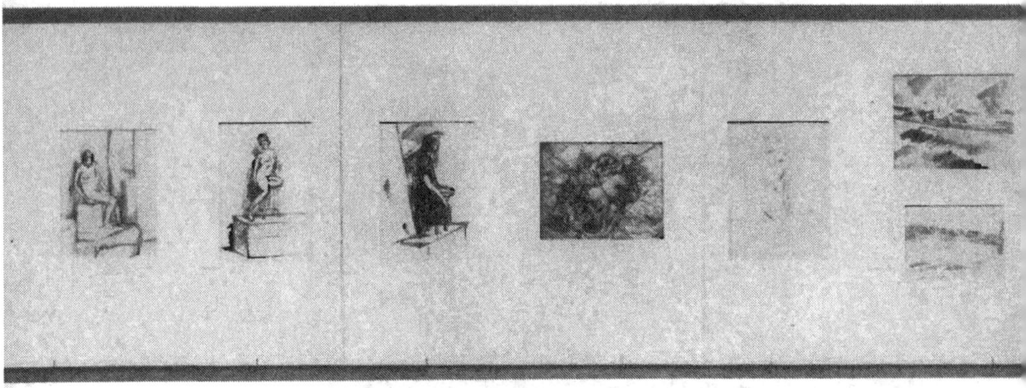

(*Top*) *Early drawings, 1898-1914.*
(*Center*) *Early portraits, 1901, 1902; Still Lifes, 1921 and 1931.*
(*Bottom*) *Portrait drawings, about 1926-27.*

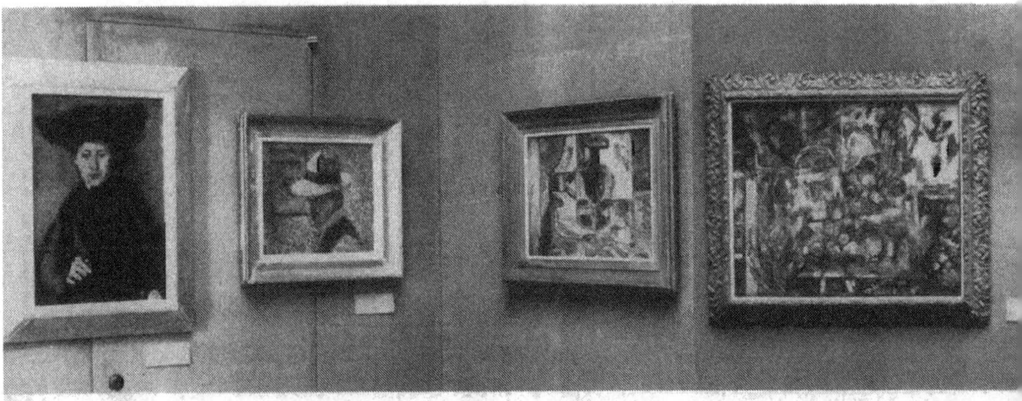

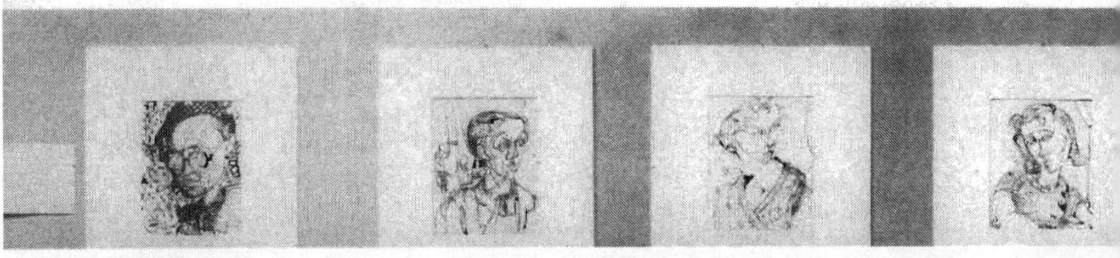

(*Above*) Drawings of St. Tropez, about 1928; California, 1930-31.
(*Below*) Provincetown landscapes; figure drawings, New York, 1932-35.

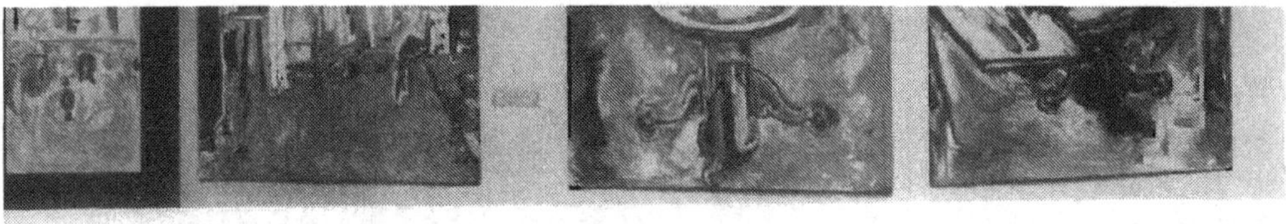

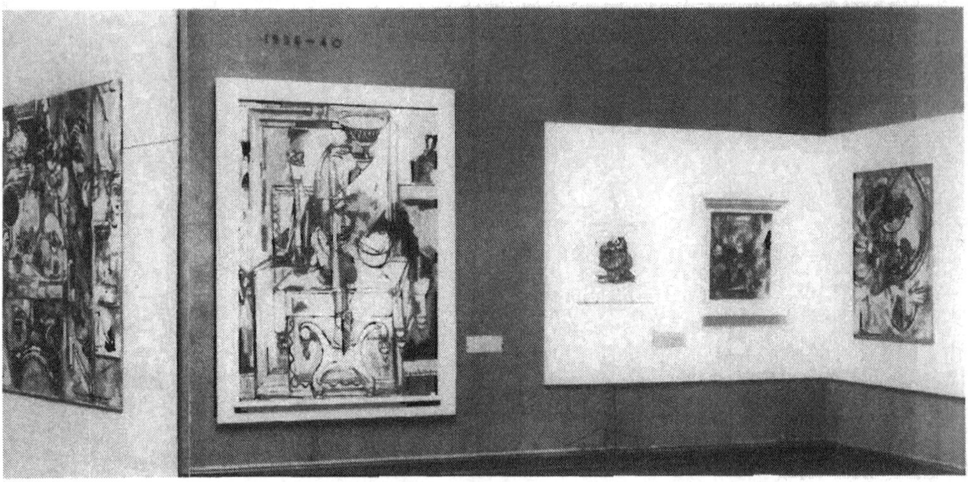

(*Above*) *Still Life painting, 1936-40.*

(*Below*) *Figure painting and landscape painting, 1935-39.*

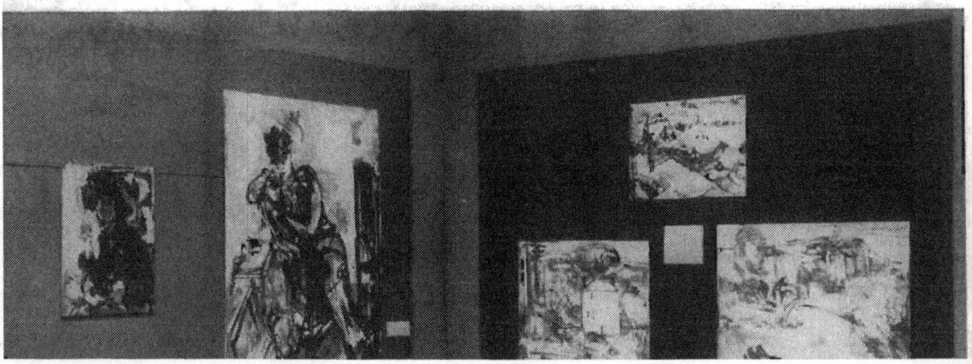

(*Top*) Still Life painting and studies, 1940-42.
(*Center*) Figure painting, 1942; Crayon landscape studies, 1941-43.
(*Bottom*) Crayon Landscape studies; Oil, "Yellow Sun," 1943.

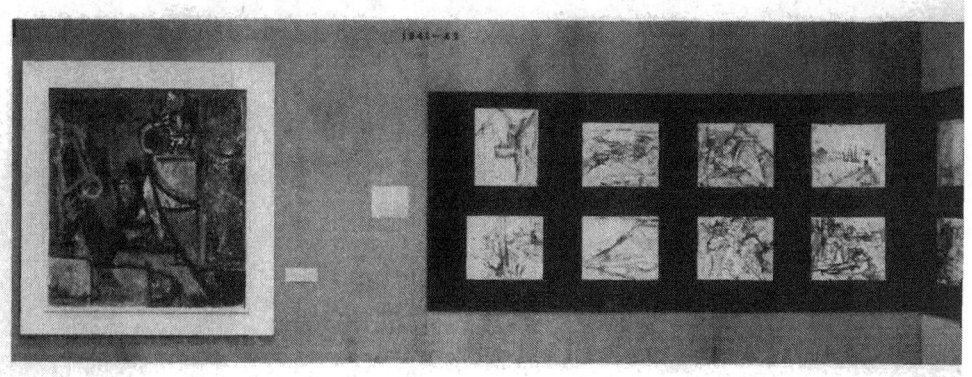

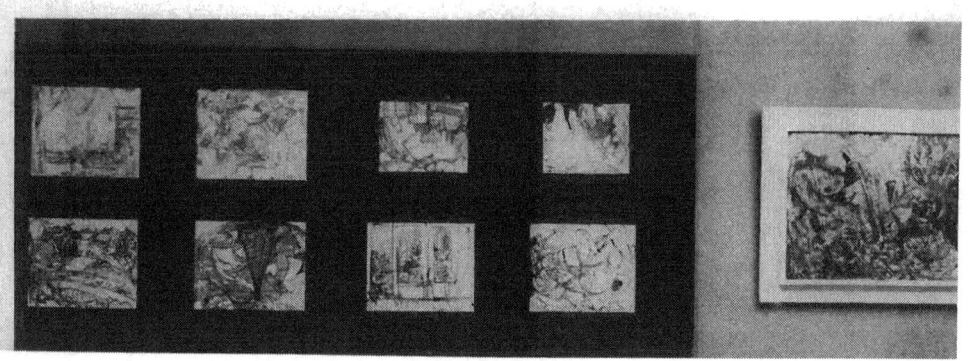

(*Top*) "*Phoenix No. 2*"; *Still Life forms, 1945-46.*

(*Center*) "*Animals in Paradise,*" *1945;* "*Nostalgia,*" *1945.*

(*Bottom*) "*Apparition,*" *1947;* "*Resolution,*" *1946;* "*Awakening,*" *1947;* "*Gray in Black in Gray,*" *1946.*

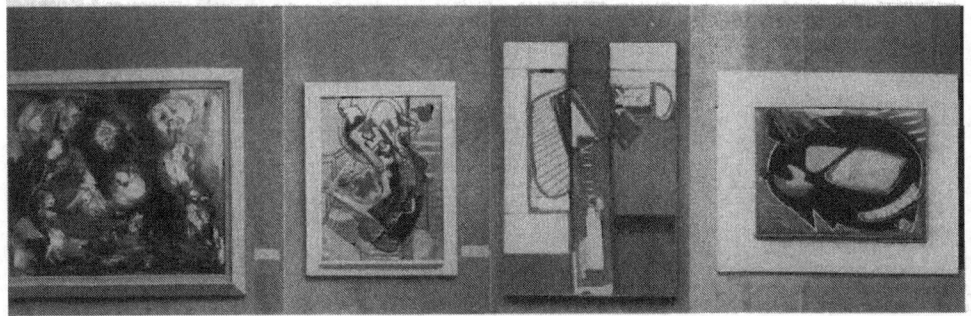

(*Above*) "White in Blue," *1947*; Drawing, *1945*; "The Circus," *1945*; "Chinese Nightingale," *1945*; "Palimpsest," *1947*; "Seated Woman," *1944*; "Abundance," *1947*; "Delight," *1947*.

(*Below*) "Submerged," *1947*; "Aggressive," *1944*.

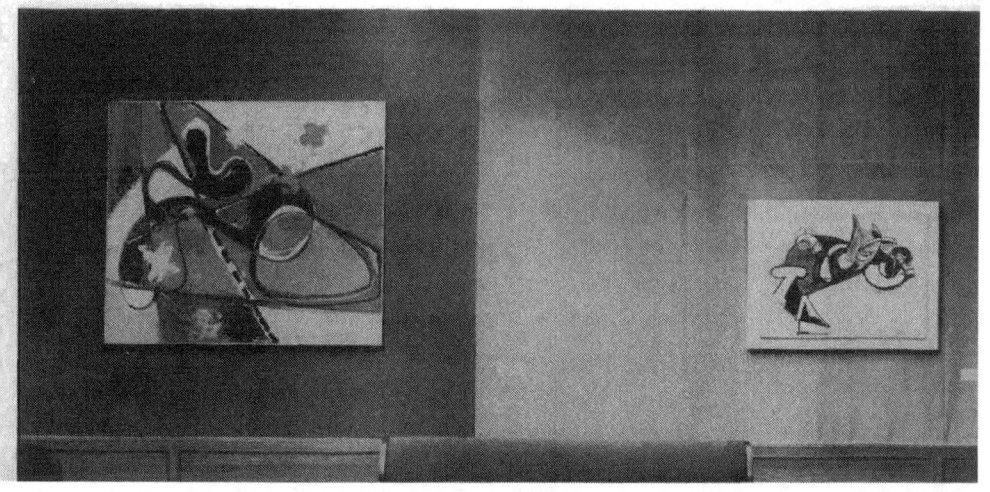

Part II: Hans Hofmann as Teacher and Philosopher

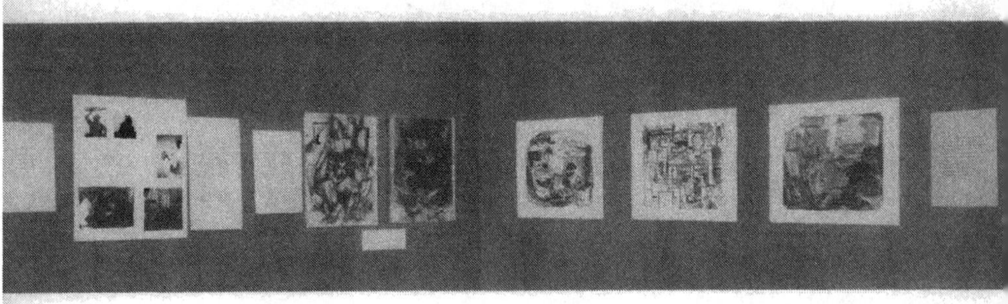

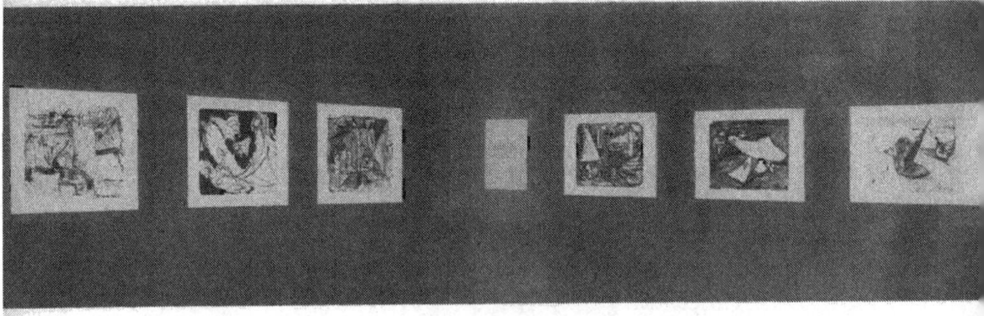

(*Top*) *Biographical data; Student drawings with criticisms in heavy black lines; Illustration of basic states of nature.*

(*Center*) *Illustration of color intervals; Color mood.*

(*Bottom*) *Illustration of the qualities of light in painting.*

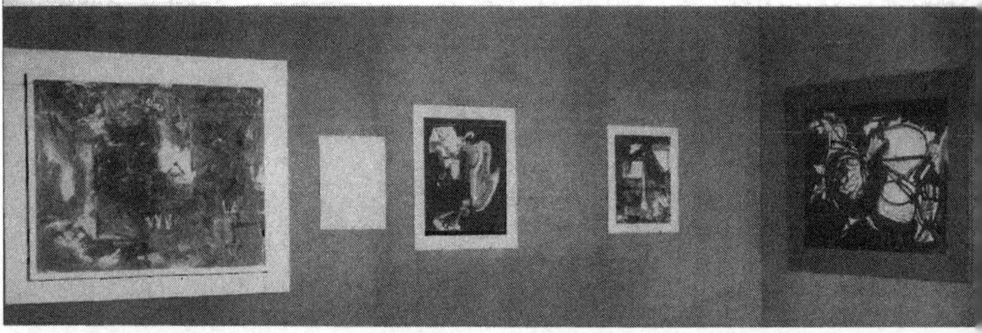

(*Top*) Distinctive forms seen in early objective work recur in later abstract pictures.

(*Center*) "Fantasia," *1945;* No title, *1946;* "Nebulous Drama," *1944;* Painting frequently develops without preconception. Titles merely define the final emotion or association of ideas.

(*Bottom*) Sequence illustrating the creation of depth in two-dimensional terms by non-naturalistic contrasts of form and color.

(*Above*) Illustration of space planes and spatial tensions; "*Nuclear*," 1947.... "*A work is endowed with inner greatness by the technical means which parallels the artist's experience and human discipline.*"

(*Below*) Illustration of simplification: "*Liberation*," 1947.. "*The ability to simplify means to eliminate the unnecessary so that the necessary may speak. Simplification is the essence of abstraction from which objective values are not necessarily eliminated.*"

HOFMANN SCHOOL, 1948

Color Notes

Page 19

Page 28

Page 29

Page 31

Page 32

Page 35

Page 35

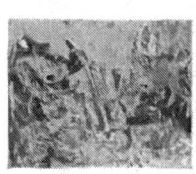
Page 36

Page 33

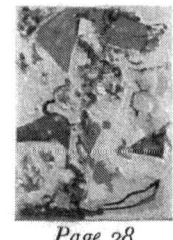
Page 38

Page 41

Page 43

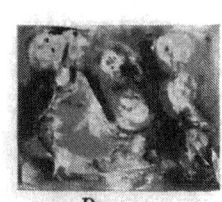
Page 45

Page 42

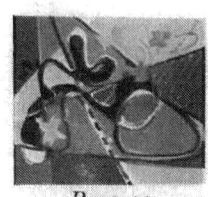
Page 44

CPSIA information can be obtained
at www.ICGtesting.com
Printed in the USA
BVHW091041171221
624286BV00008B/221